THE STORY OF

DAN
BRIGHT

crime, corruption and injustice
in the crescent city

D0104544

University of New Orleans Press
Manufactured in the United States of America
All rights reserved
ISBN: 978-1-60801-124-7

Book and cover design: Alex Dimeff

Library of Congress Cataloging-in-Publication Data

Names: Bright, Dan (Daniel L.), author. | Nobel, Justin, author.
Title: The story of Dan Bright / by Dan Bright, as told to Justin Nobel.
Description: New Orleans : University of New Orleans Press, [2016] |
Includes bibliographical references and index.
Identifiers: LCCN 2016014257 | ISBN 9781608011247 (pbk. : alk. paper)
Subjects: LCSH: Bright, Dan (Daniel L.) | Death row
inmates--Louisiana--Biography. | African American
prisoners--Louisiana--Biography. | Judicial error--Louisiana. | Criminal
justice, Administration of--Louisiana. | Discrimination in criminal
justice administration--Louisiana.
Classification: LCC HV8701.B75 A3 2016 | DDC 364.152/3092 [B] --dc23
LC record available at https://lccn.loc.gov/2016014257

This is a work of nonfiction. The author has drawn from a number of sources, including media articles and investigations, legal transcripts, and interviews. It is also a memoir, which is to say that the story, the experiences, and the words are the author's alone. Dialogue has been re-created from memory. Names of certain characters have been changed to protect their privacy.

THE UNIVERSITY OF NEW ORLEANS PRESS
unopress.org

THE STORY OF

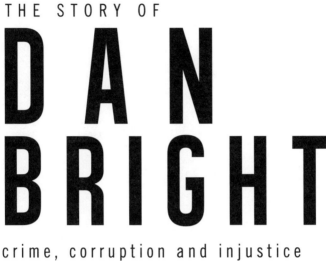

DAN
BRIGHT

crime, corruption and injustice
in the crescent city

as told by dan bright to justin nobel
foreword by clive stafford smith

"Remember especially that you cannot be the judge of anyone. For there can be no judge of a criminal on earth until the judge knows that he, too, is a criminal, exactly the same as the one who stands before him, and that he is perhaps most guilty of all for the crime of the one standing before him. When he understands this, then he will be able to be a judge. However mad that may seem, it is true."

—Fyodor Dostoyevsky

ACKNOWLEDGEMENTS

Dan would like to thank his mother, his sister, his children, the staff of the Innocence Project New Orleans and the Louisiana Capital Assistance Center, Morrison & Foerster, Ben Cohen, Clive Stafford Smith, Gary Wainwright, Justin Nobel, and UNO Press.

FOREWORD

The document we had uncovered astounded me. It was entirely blacked out except for the sentence that read:

> "The source further advised that Dan Bright, *aka* Poonie, is in jail for the murder committed by ——"

This single sheet of paper, reflecting fewer than twenty words, was proof positive that Dan was telling the truth: that he was innocent of the murder of Murray Barnes on Superbowl Sunday, January 29th, 1995. But it was also, in equal parts, horrifying: it meant that the foremost federal law enforcement agency in the country had known he was likely innocent and had been covering up the evidence. The reference to Dan being in *jail*, rather than in prison, was significant: it meant that their source had told them this before Dan's trial had even begun, since he was being held in pretrial detention ("jail") at the time.

The document in question came to us through an FBI Freedom of Information Act request made by my colleague Ben Cohen, long after Dan had been sentenced to death. And yet the Bureau saw fit to black out the name of the real killer before sending Ben the document. They refused to tell us who actually did the crime.

When depicted by Hollywood, FBI G-men spend their working hours seeking justice, chasing down variants of Al Capone. Here, in the surreal world of New Orleans, they were sitting on information that the wrong man was waiting to die in a cell up at Angola, the Louisiana State Penitentiary, built on a former plantation and named for the country from which most of the slaves had been seized. The FBI had held on tight to the evidence until forced to turn it over by federal law. Even then, some faceless FBI bureaucrat had redacted the name of the true killer from the FBI 302, the form used to record statements taken by Special Agents from the Bureau from witnesses.

Ben Cohen and I were representing Dan Bright in the appeal of his conviction and death sentence. We set about trying to force a little justice, but those who are given authority over life and death are sometimes immune to common sense. We asked the state court to issue a subpoena to the FBI to appear in the Orleans Parish Criminal District Court and produce the original and unredacted 302. But there is a strange rule, the "Touhy rule," created by the federal government, which allows the Bureau simply to refuse to comply with a state court order. There is no justice in such an act. It is merely a matter of the might of the federal government over the state courts. The FBI duly invoked the "Touhy rule" and removed the legal fight about the subpoena from the Orleans Parish courtroom to federal district court.

It was here that Dan was finally able to tread his first step towards freedom. The federal judge demanded to know why the government was keeping the name of the real murderer secret. The government argued that it was necessary to protect the man's "privacy" interests. I remember the judge snorting rather overtly before he ordered immediate disclosure of the name that had been redacted, the name of the real killer of Murray Barnes. Despite this, it would be years before Dan was a free man.

Let me reveal my prejudice: I really like Dan. I always have since he was a twenty-six-year-old in his death row cell. With his owlish steel-rimmed spectacles, he looked more like a college fraternity brother than someone who was waiting to die on Louisiana's lethal injection gurney. In his book, he is overly kind to me. More of the credit should go to Ben Cohen, who did the lion's share of the work; to Kathleen Hawke-Norman, the former juror who fought for his freedom; and to Innocence Project New Orleans (www.ip-no.org). But the time I spent trying to salvage some of Dan's life taught me some important lessons about the legal system, and about life itself. The book you hold in your hands details many of the lessons Dan's story gave me; it is as much an insight into the mindset of law enforcement as it is into the story of Dan Bright.

It was ultimately clear what motivated the police: they believed Dan made his living selling drugs, and they thought they were justified in eliminating him any way they could. In other words, the law enforcement officers had no compunction when it came to breaking the law if they felt it was necessary, and—again—the might of law enforcement ultimately dictated what they considered was right.

Dan was indeed a drug dealer, at a time when record numbers of his peers were either dying in drug turf wars or going to prison. He is very open about it through the first half of the book. He chose his profession because ultimately he was born into a world of economic disadvantage and racial profiling. At the age of fifteen, he already knew that the American dream was a myth. He was never going to escape the Florida Project in New Orleans with a college degree. He knew at a young age that he did not fall in the fraction of a percent of African-American males who would achieve fame and fortune through sporting prowess. But he knew enough about the American capitalist system to spot a market opportunity in the drug business. Somebody was going to play the game—in much the same way as hedge fund managers make vast sums of money by gambling with stocks and shares—and it may as well be him.

At the time of his conviction, and even today, that Dan was a drug dealer was enough to justify his execution to many in law enforcement and the public at large. In the era when Dan operated, the U.S.A.'s War on Drugs directed law enforcement to target participants in the drug trade. It was not always thus. I spoke with various members of the notorious Medellin Cartel in the course of one recent case. Some were upper-middle class Colombians, and they described how they originally got into the drug trade thinking it was the next big thing—the next big *legal* thing. It was the War on Drugs that criminalized the trade to the extent seen in Dan's story. In contemporary times, it can be a strange era to look back on—now, even a conservative paper like London *Times* recently argued that the war had been lost and called for decriminalization of all drugs.

By the time the legal system turned its attentions on him, Dan never stood a chance. He had frittered away most of his money, but his mother was still able to scrape together $5,000 to pay for a private attorney, the late Robert Oberfell. This probably saved his life in the end – not because the man was better than one of the court-appointed public defenders, but because he was even worse. Oberfell met Dan just once before trial, did no preparation, and turned up drunk on the morning of what turned out to be Dan's one-day trial.

Dan was ironically, fabulously fortunate to get sentenced to death, rather than to life without parole. Do-gooders like Ben and me only had the resources to offer free legal help to those on Death Row. Stretched thin, we could at least help Dan and the 80 others who were slated for execution. This fact is particularly painful considering that the prisoners serving life without parole in this, the largest prison in the United States of America, were going to die in Angola as well, joining the others buried in the prison grave yard, with the crosses marking their burials etched with just a prison number.

Since the death penalty was reintroduced in the 1970s, there have been ten exonerations of men on Louisiana's death row, against 28 executions. That means a condemned person has a good chance of being proven innocent and liberated. Applying the same statistics to the rest of the 6,300 prisoners, you'd expect hundreds to be proven innocent – but such will never be the case, as those languishing in Angola have no right to free counsel and must almost inevitably fight on alone for their freedom. The only exception is the bolt of lightning provided by Innocence Project New Orleans, a tiny charity devoted to redressing mis-carriages of justice for those serving a sentence "lon-ger" than death. IPNO's record is remarkable, perhaps the best of any innocence project nationwide, as they have achieved the release of 28 innocent people in what is, in my experience, the toughest jurisdiction in the country – but have scores more prisoners on their books waiting for their help.

Dan's case taught me many other lessons. What is called "prosecutorial" or "police misconduct" is, sad to say, all too common in capital cases. I was not sur-prised that the FBI would struggle gamely to keep an innocent man on death row. But I had never paused to think what impact this would have on the jurors who had been tasked with deciding Dan's fate. It was in dealing with the jurors that I met the remarkable Kathleen Hawk Norman – a white Republican woman who had been the elected foreperson of the jury that had convicted Dan and sentenced him to death. At a deeply personal level, she felt betrayed by the officials who had hidden evidence from her when they asked that she dispense justice, even if it meant taking a fellow citizen's life – and twice-betrayed when the same officials refused to set the matter straight. As the book progresses, Dan describes the remarkable battle she waged for him. Admittedly, I cannot recall the terror she inspired in the trial judge without a smile. He started proceedings earlier and earlier each day he sat on the case, in a futile effort to get things over with before Kathleen could sweep into his courtroom.

I have several keepsakes from Dan's ordeal: chief among them are the lessons Dan taught me about our justice system, which are laid out in the pages of this book. Dan also gave me the watch that he wore in prison, which he was only too happy to get rid of after nine years of watching the seconds tick by in what is perhaps America's most feared institution. And I have the ten-dollar check that Dan was given as he walked out of the prison gates, representing $1.11 for each year he spent serving a sentence for a crime he did not commit.

—*Clive Stafford Smith, June 2016*

The day of the trial my lawyer was drunk. I could smell it on his breath. This guy was wearing his usual rundown shoes and an old rented-ass suit, papers falling all over the place. After 16 months in the Parish prison he only visited me once, two days before the trial started, and he stayed for just 20 minutes. The whole neighborhood knew I was innocent. An FBI informant had actually witnessed another man commit the murder. And the state's star witness had been drinking for 12 hours straight the night of the crime.

They picked the jury before lunch. On it was a former undercover cop, a current employee of the New Orleans Police Department. In a single day, I was convicted of first-degree murder. The next day, again before lunch, I was sentenced to death. Now I am in the back of a squad car surrounded by police officers. My legs are shackled, my wrists are handcuffed, and officers have put an electrical restraining belt around my waist. I am one of the first people they are using this piece of equipment on, and one officer keeps joking about hitting the button. Speeding away from New Orleans, the lights of the squad car flashing, I am thinking: *How long is it going to be before I see this city again?*

As we get closer to the Louisiana State Penitentiary at Angola, I see how everyone is living in trailers up on a hill, with cows and horses. At the entrance gate, prison guards are waiting, ten redneck types. When I say redneck, I don't just mean white. A redneck is anyone who talks about hunting alligators and eating raccoons and squirrel and is always spitting everywhere. These rednecks walk me to a big white building surrounded by high fences. Guys are planting flowers and cutting grass, making it beautiful, and just inside this gate is the execution chamber. Death row is on a hill, and the rest of the prison is down in a big old ditch. It looks more like a farm than a prison. You feel like you're traveling back in time to slavery days or even before that, to the days of Roman gladiators.

Guards strip off my clothing and make me open my mouth, lift up my testicles and cough, bend over so they can look in my rectum, and lift up my feet so they can see under my toes.

"If you get executed," says one guard, "who do you want them to send your personal belongings to?"

"I'm going to take them to hell with me," I snap. They look at me and say nothing.

I am escorted to C-Tier, down a long concrete hallway, to cell #12. There is an iron toilet, an iron sink, an iron bunk with a thin little mattress, and there is a tiny table that attaches to the wall with a built-in stool. We have two foot lockers for our belongings, and I unload my things, family photos, my legal work, a few books.

"Who's in cell 12?" someone a few cells down yells.

I don't reply. I don't want to build a relationship with someone who is going to be executed. I am still convinced that things will get straightened out, that I will be released. I sit there on that little mattress and I think. I go back to the beginning. Back to the city that was my home, the city that had formed me, the city that had framed me, wrongfully convicted me of murder and sent me to Angola to be executed. But my story is complicated. This city nourished me, and I had become a part of it, and it wasn't always a good part. Despite everything, it was the city that I loved, and the city where almost all of the people I have ever known and loved lived.

Chapter One

The City Explained

I came up in the Florida Projects during the 1970s and 1980s, one of the most violent times in the history of New Orleans. Florida was a bunch of three story brick buildings developed for whites after World War II. Initially, black people weren't allowed in. Then the blacks moved in, and the government let the projects fall apart. You could see that at one time it was a nice place to live, but no more. Florida was one of the most violent projects in the city and the poorest. The pool was broke, the swings were broke, and there was bottle glass broken all over the playground. Everything a kid needed to enjoy himself didn't work. No flowers, no trees, just dirt and concrete. People walking around with no shoes on their feet, people going without eating, no heat, no water, the lights go out and it's cold, guys selling drugs, shootings, drinking, prostitution. Every time you hear gunshots, you gotta lay on the floor. It's a routine your parents teach you at a young age. I remember going to school one morning when I was real young, and there being a dead body in the stairwell. A man had been shot in the head. That wasn't a big deal. All you do is walk over it, go on to school, mind your own business.

When I got in a car and went uptown, on St. Charles Street or around the lakefront, I would see everyone living totally different. Kids driving around in nice sports cars their parents bought for them. I remember one kid's parents bought him a Camaro T-top with shiny rims. He played football, if I'm not mistaken. All the girls loved him, loved his material things, and they'd follow him around. Guys like this would drive over to their girl's house, pick them up, go play tennis. Yeah, I thought I could get along with them. But later on, the more I got to know these kids, the more I realized that they took everything for granted. I would just look at them and think, you all have no idea what is going on in this world, and you know nothing about New Orleans. In New Orleans, everyday someone is killed. And the only time they would know that is if their parents watched the news.

When we were young, my pops used to take me and my little brother and sister to see Al Copeland's house, the man who started Popeye's Chicken. He was a big celebrity around New Orleans, and every Christmas he lit his house up with all sorts of lights. It was so perfect, lights everywhere, reindeer, Santa Clauses. My brother and sister were overwhelmed by the lights, but I wasn't excited about that. I was trying to figure out how I can get a house like that, screw those lights. Maybe that is where it started, I don't know. I wanted that success. I wanted that power. New Orleans is like crabs in a bucket, everyone is trying to make it out. Everyone is trying to get something, and no one is going to let someone else take anything from them. I had two parents, I had clothes on my back but I wanted another life. I enjoyed the street life. I wanted to do what the old gangsters were doing, but do it better. I wouldn't say it was forced on me, but I grew up in it, and I was good at it.

My two best friends were Lucky and Romeo. Lucky was short and stocky, like a bulldog, and very intelligent. He was a bookworm like me and always walking around with a little book in his pocket. People picked on Lucky, and he fought back with his mind. "Hey ugly-ass," someone would say, and Lucky would reply, "Bet I can spell better than you!" In the Projects, Lucky lived directly below me. I'd knock on the floor with a broomstick to get his attention, and we'd meet outside. Romeo lived across the way. He was tall and slim, one of those pretty boy types. Romeo wasn't that educated book-wise, but streetwise he was. He came up poor, maybe six brothers, six sisters. Romeo was Creole. His people were from Lafayette. Me and Lucky used to go by his house to get him, and we'd hear his mother and father talking in French. I wanted to learn it, but he never wanted us to hear that. Romeo pretended he wasn't Creole. He liked to be black. They were the only two people in the city I truly trusted.

They were also my business partners. At elementary school, you had kids from the Projects, like us,

and then you had *house boys*. They lived in houses in
the Lower 9th Ward, on the other side of the Industrial
Canal. House boys weren't rich, but they were richer
than us, and they came to school with candy. Now
and Laters, Snickers bars, M & Ms, this candy called
Whatchamacallit. They gave it to us because they
wanted to be in our little group, then we sold it back
to them. Later we started selling cigarettes, a dime a
piece. Our spot was behind the school. A few other
guys tried selling there, but we let them know it was
our thing. We wouldn't let anyone else sell nothing,
uh-uh, we weren't gonna let them profit off what we
started. If guys tried, we jumped them. It didn't matter
if they were older than us. We used sticks, whatever we
could get our hands on. From an early age I knew, you
had to control the market.

Our elementary school was Johnson C. Lockett, a
pretty decent school for a public school. At some point,
the little girls started calling me Poonie, and it stuck.
I don't remember any of my teachers. Elementary
school was a business opportunity. The school was
safe because it wasn't in the Projects, like five blocks
away. But you could still hear the shots coming from
the Projects. Sometimes the gunshots were real close,
and it sounded like they were right inside the classroom.
The house boys didn't know what to do. Gunshots were
something strange to them. For the Project kids, stray
bullets were business as usual. We knew the bullets
weren't meant for us. Back in the Projects, we'd learn the
story, and the next day, we'd tell the teacher and house
boys, "Hey, you heard those shots, this what happened..."

The big corners in our Project were Law and Congress and Law and Desire, and my family lived right in between, on the corner of Law and Gallier. So, one block away you had Congress and just down the street was Desire. We were in the heart of everything, and I looked out my window and watched it all. As a kid, that window was my television, and the streets were my cartoons. I could look outside and see gangsters, drug dealers, pimps, prostitutes. It fascinated me, but at the same time, I saw the mistakes the older guys were making. Why did they dress with all their fancy jewelry? Why did they have their fancy car parked on the avenue where they were selling? Why not put it around the corner, why not be as discreet as possible? You can't blend in if you're standing out. Even as a kid, I noticed the little business mistakes people were making.

I was lucky. I grew up in a two-parent household with a younger brother and younger sister. My father drove trucks, mostly local runs, but sometimes long distances. My mother stayed home and took care of us. On Fridays she wouldn't cook anything because my father got paid, and we went to Burger King. It was about two miles, and we took the car, my mother and father, me, and my little sister and little brother. Driving there everyone else would be all excited, talking with each other. I'd be looking out the window, in my own world. I was trying to figure out how I was gonna make some money, what kind of candy I was gonna sell the next day at school, or what kind of cigarettes. I was part of the family, but I was never a part of the family. I was more into myself.

My father was a square guy. He came from an upper class family and grew up in a house in the Lower 9th Ward. On my father's side, you had not one lawbreaker. Everyone was college grads, doctors, business owners. My father used to take my brother and I to see his people in the Lower 9th, or on fishing trips, or to car racing shows. I never wanted to go, but my little brother went. He liked to spend time with my pops, and my father began to take my little brother's side more because of that. I didn't care. The more time he spent with him the less he bothered me, and the more time I had to run around the Projects. I preferred to hang with my uncles than hang with my father. I just always wanted to get back to the Projects. The Projects was my family. It was like a big old reunion every day.

Each Project is its own world. We had this one kid named Baba who had never been out of the Projects, never went down Canal Street, never went to Mardi Gras. He had a big family and a lot of brothers, and they would bring him clothes and the things he needed from the outside world. There were others like him. Why'd they never leave? Because they were comfortable in the Projects. They felt safe there. They didn't have to be somebody they weren't. People say that if you have a fancy job, you have to be comfortable in that fancy job, and to do that you have to change your attitude, your vocabulary, your dress code. But in the Projects, you don't have to change anything. You just have to be yourself. As long as you weren't trying to hurt someone, people would take you in. You could go into any house, take a nap, get some food, use the restroom, and come back out.

My father never really got the hang of inner city life. He went to work, came home, and went inside. Wake up, go to work, come home, same routine every day. He never hung outside, he never socialized. He never approved of the project life. He grew up under a different set of rules, and I never accepted those rules. My father and I had the type of relationship where I knew he loved me and I loved him, but we didn't hug, we didn't say it. Even at a young age, we didn't talk much, just, "Hey, what's up, how ya doing?" That type of thing. My pops believed, "He is a man, he can take care of himself."

My pops was a stubborn man. He didn't want nobody doing nothing for him. He changed his oil in the yard just so he could do it himself. My pops also believed in physical punishment, and I wasn't for that. Man, I would catch an ass whopping. Would I call him an abusive father? I don't know. I was much closer to my mother's family. Her side was the opposite. My mother grew up in the Florida Projects, partying, hanging out, going to concerts and clubs, the inner city life. My mother was Baptist. She had three brothers and four sisters, plus she had cousins and aunties and great aunties living in the Projects. On my mother's side, you had alcoholics, armed robbers, hustlers. There were a lot of barrooms up and down where I lived, and at 9 and 10, I used to sneak in there to find her. She'd run me out, "What you want?!" My father's family was strict Jehovah's Witnesses and thought my mother was low class. They didn't even come to the wedding, and they never approved of her.

I have to say, though, my father provided for us. We had everything kids were supposed to have: clothes on our back, food, pets, toys, bikes. Other kids were jealous. Some kids, if they had a father, had to wait for the father to come home to eat. My mother didn't play that. She made sure to feed us right away. We came inside, washed our hands, then she fixed us something, chicken, pork chops, steak. It wasn't real steak like at the restaurant, it was little bitty steaks. We had smoked sausage, pickled pig tips, cabbage, spaghetti, red beans, white beans, all kinds of beans. I liked the beans. I never did like cabbage. I never did like spaghetti. "I'm not cooking just for you, you not special enough to eat your own thing," my mother would say. "You eat what I cook, or you get yourself a sandwich out of the ice box, or you starve."

My mother took people in who didn't have enough to eat. She knew which kids were hungry because she knew their mothers, and she knew the ways of their mothers. That's how it was, at age 10 these kids had no food because their mothers were spending it on drugs. Food stamps only come once a month, when they come they're gone in a week. Or mothers sold their food stamps for drugs. Kids in my neighborhood would have loved to be in my shoes, in my household. Even if we weren't rich, we had more than the average family. If you were to walk inside our apartment, you'd forget you were in the Projects. We had food on the stove, the house was clean, and because my pops got used furniture from rich people after he made deliveries, we had nice furniture.

I don't know how much there is to say about my little brother and sister. I got along with my sister. She was my little sister, and I looked out for her. As far as my little brother goes, we fought over everything, even small things. There was always a tension. Why? I don't know. We just bumped heads. Other kids came to our house to play, mostly with him. I was more into hanging out with the older guys. I never did want to be a kid. I never wanted to be treated like a kid. I always wanted to be older than I was. When I was small, my mom would go to put my shoes on, but I wanted to put my own shoes on. I wanted to show her I could do it myself. If she put my shoes on for me, that would signify that she was treating me like a baby, and I didn't want to be treated like that.

Do I regret my childhood? No, I don't regret it. Some kids enjoy their childhood, some kids don't have a childhood, and some kids have one but don't want one.

My typical day as a kid: I would wake up on my own, get dressed, and figure out how Romeo, Lucky, and I were gonna make some money. What type of candy was hot, or how to get some cigarettes to sell. My mother walked me and my sister and brother to school. This may sound strange, but my mother was one of the most beautiful women in the Projects. She was very tall, much taller than my father, and she was a nice dresser. She stayed neat, classy. Walking to school was like a fashion show. All the guys flirted with her. Everywhere she went, she got attention, and I didn't like that. She dressed my brother and I like twins and, we looked nice too, and my sister looked nice. At school, Romeo, Lucky, and I did our thing, made some money. After school, come home. I still had to do my homework. Then go outside. But I wasn't allowed to hang by our place because all that drug activity was going down. My mother sent me around the corner, where my grandmother lived.

My grandmother was like my second mother, and she stuck up for me. She called me Scooter. "Scooter wouldn't do that," she'd say. I got what I wanted, and she wouldn't let nobody whoop or punish me. If someone said something negative about me, she wouldn't believe them. My grandmother had a four-bedroom apartment with my uncle and aunties. All my uncles' friends would hang out there, all my aunties' friends, my cousins. My grandmother was the type of person who would take people in and feed them, that's where my mother got it from. Could be three in the morning, she would take them in. She was like the big mama of the Projects. Someone needed somewhere to stay, go over there and stay on that floor, and she'd fix something for you. Women, men, young, old. For Christmas or Thanksgiving, everyone came to her house for a big old feast, soul food. Me and my grandmother loved custard pie. She went to the bakery and got three or four custard pies. If someone tried to take a piece, she'd say, "Don't touch that pie, that's Scooter's pie!"

My grandmother was also a realist. She knew how hard it was growing up in the Projects. I remember later on, when I was giving her money, someone asked her, "Why you taking that dirty money?"

"Where it dirty at," my grandmother said, "let me wash it off." And she went into the washing room, "It ain't gonna be dirty when I get through with it."

Every week my grandmother went to church. When I was small, I went, but later I stopped, and she didn't push. The older folks had their church, and if that's what they believed, who was I to stop them? But even as a kid, I was turned off from religion. I had seen what people can do with religion. I had seen preachers say a few scriptures just to get folks out of their money. I had seen preachers drive up in nice cars bought with other people's savings. I had seen preachers with different women, preachers with prostitutes. I had seen one of the neighborhood drug dealers all of a sudden get the Holy Spirit or the holy whatever in him and become a preacher. The way I saw it, he was still taking people's money and giving them a drug. At a young age, I realized, uh-uh, church ain't for me. But my grandmother went to church every week and bingo every night. On Sunday she'd come home from church, change clothes, and get something to eat, then go back for bingo.

It was my mother who forced me to become independent. For example, at Burger King, she made us read the menu and order ourselves. That way we learned how to conduct ourselves in public, how to talk, how to speak. My mother was the type who always made sure we knew who the president was, the vice president, the governor, important things. I didn't talk that much, but my mother knew I was the strongest out of the kids. When she had to go somewhere, she put me in charge. Even at 9 and 10-years-old, I did errands for her. She gave me a piece of paper with our home phone number and my name, walked me to the bus stop, and put me on the Desire bus to go buy school shoes for my brother and sister.

The Desire bus ran from the 9th Ward all the way to Canal Street. My mother told the bus driver where to stop, and she'd write down the sizes on a piece of paper to give to the man at the store. "Make sure I get my change back," she'd tell me, and I'd drive across the city all by myself. Everyone disagreed with her. "Why you sending that boy way up there?" The bus could be dangerous. There was a store right before the Projects where the drivers stopped to use the bathroom, and a few times these guys with masks came on while the driver was gone and robbed everyone. Still my mother put me on that bus.

Those trips are how I learned the city. I got off the bus and did what I had to do, but once I had purchased the shoes or whatever it was I needed to get, the rest was on me. I walked around Canal Street, went into Woolworth's, got a donut. I saw things I wasn't supposed to see. I walked around Bourbon Street, peeped about. People stared. "Look at this little kid with these shopping bags coming off Canal Street!" I saw the guys with nice business suits and nice briefcases walking around. I was fascinated by that world and admired it from afar. The corporate world, power. But I was also fascinated by the street world. The businessmen with their suits and the real gangsters in the Projects.

I knew one thing, no matter where I saw that Desire bus, it was going to get me home. The bus came through the 8th Ward and back to the 9th, and once I got to the 9th Ward, I could get off anywhere because that was my neighborhood. Someone would always know me. Like I said, I had a very big family back in the Projects, so no one was going to do nothing. You would have had to hurt me to get those shopping bags out of my hands.

One day I was walking back from the bus, and my uncles were hanging outside. The police pulled up, and one guy panicked and threw a bundle down. A bundle was 25 bags of heroin or cocaine, at $25 a bag. The police lined everyone up against the wall. I had seen who threw the drugs, and maybe they figured by me being about ten years old, I would be the weakest link. The cops put me in the back of the police car and tried to scare me into telling them, but I wouldn't tell. In my neighborhood, no matter how young you were, you knew that the police were wrong, period. The police were bad people to us.

"Who threw the drugs down?" the police officers asked me.

"I dunno," I said. "I didn't see nothing."

I still had my shopping bags with me from being downtown. All my mother knew was that I was supposed to be coming home. Someone must have told her what had happened because eventually she came outside and started fussing with the police.

"He needs to tell us who threw down the drugs," the officer told her.

"No, he don't!" my mother said. "That's not his job to tell you." She was furious.

"We were just gonna scare him," the officer pleaded.

"You are just gonna take him out of that car!" my mother snapped back. And they did. After that, everything changed.

From that day on, all the older guys knew I could be trusted not to snitch, and they started asking me to do things for them. One of my uncle's friends, this older guy named Goldy, took a particular liking to me.

"Come on, Poon," guys would say, "take this and put it over there." Or, "Hey Poon, drop this in the trash can over there for this guy."

When I did it, I would come back with my hand open, "Where's my money?" You tell me to do something I want my cut.

Goldy would laugh. "Give him his cut."

CHAPTER TWO

MENTORSHIP

At first Goldy handed me drugs through my bedroom window, and I held them for him. When he had a lot of stuff, sometimes I held it for him right in school. Say he had more than one bundle, say he had five bundles, I'd take three bundles with me to school and put them in my bag. Later in the day when he needed more stuff, Goldy went to school and told my teacher he had to talk with me. He'd take the bundles and leave me the money. The more Goldy let me hold, the more I saw, and the more I saw, the more I wanted. I was making $50, a lot of money for an 11 year-old in the 1970s. Still he was making $1,500.

"Give me something to sell for myself," I told Goldy. And he did.

I think me asking made him proud. He saw I wouldn't settle for crumbs. Goldy started me with bags of weed. I sold after school let out and on weekends.

Romeo and Lucky saw all this money and knew I wasn't getting it from selling candy. When I told them what I was doing, they wanted in, but Goldy didn't want to deal with Lucky and Romeo. He didn't know what would happen if the police caught them, if they would snitch or not. Goldy also didn't want their mothers finding out he was giving them drugs to hold. He told me he didn't want to meet them.

"They're friends," I pleaded. "You accept me, you accept them!"

"No, it don't work like that," Goldy said. "They *your* friends, you deal with them."

So Goldy gave me the stuff, and I passed it on to Romeo and Lucky. We hung out in the stairwells of our building in the projects. I might be in the front stairwell, and Romeo would be in the back stairwell. Lucky might be walking around the building, making sure we didn't get caught. We took turns. Someone says police are coming, and we'd run inside Lucky's apartment. Lucky's mother left early for a housekeeping job downtown so we basically had his place to ourselves. That was the beginning.

A lot of kids our age were jealous. Others were infatuated. They wanted in. But they couldn't do the things we were doing. Because I looked like some square, nerdy-type kid, I was underestimated. No one imagined I was doing the things I was doing. Lucky and I gave some kids money for food or school clothes. We felt sorry for them. We knew how it was. But Romeo didn't have any sympathy. He had a chip on his shoulder. Poor kids just made him mad. "Look at what we're doing!" he said. "That's why we have money, we're working, we're hustling."

I had my days when I didn't want to be bothered with Romeo, but he was like a brother to me, and I was going to stick with him to the end. He was cruel, and he did dumb shit, but when the smoke cleared, I knew he would be there for me, and I was there for him. I recall I had saved up like $300 or $400, and my mother needed money for something. My pops was trying to figure out where to get it. I kept the cash in an Adidas shoebox under my bed, and I went in there and got my mother some money. "You know what you're doing, boy?" she asked me later. I told her yes, and she never asked again. Being from the streets, she knew. The streets talked. I don't think she knew how much or how heavy I was into it, but she knew I was doing something. One day she was walking me to school, and we stopped at the store. One of these older gangsters came up to me, "What's up, little Poonie!" I swear I saw her smile.

"I can't stop you, huh," she said. She was proud of me for becoming a man at that young age. Maybe it was wrong, I don't know, but you have to remember, my mother came up with my life, she knew what it was like growing up as a kid in the Projects. And besides, Goldy was family to us, she trusted him and knew he wouldn't do anything to hurt me. My pops never understood what was happening in my life, and he certainly didn't approve of me dealing drugs as an 11- and 12-year-old. We basically stopped speaking.

My pops wasn't the type to sit me down and talk about what path to take. Everything with him was physical, and for a while, I faulted my mother for that. She was my guardian angel, but she never stopped him from hitting me. I don't know if she figured that this is what a father was supposed to do or what, but more and more, I withdrew from the family. My intention was always to leave, though I never intended to leave that early. But a particular incident occurred. I had some money saved up, and I had some drugs, all in different shoeboxes under the bed. Way under the bed. One day I came home from school, and the shoeboxes were gone, my father had found everything. He hit me, and that was it, I left home. And I got a gun from Romeo.

Because Romeo was a pretty boy, people picked on him. He didn't have the muscles or the build other kids did, so he learned how to retaliate in other ways. He liked weapons. First it was a razor blade, which he kept in his belt, then a knife, then a gun. Every time someone was selling a gun in the Projects, Romeo would buy it. He just loved guns. I didn't want to shoot my pops, so I shot his car, the whole car, the headlights, the windshield, everything. Then I left. Lucky and Romeo left home, too. Lucky's mother was too busy working to worry about him moving out. And Romeo had issues with his own father, who worked at a Chevrolet factory. He'd come home and beat Romeo's mother. It made Romeo furious. One day he pulled a gun on his father and left. Me, Lucky, and Romeo moved to East Orleans.

At that time, anyone with money was in the East: lawyers, judges, businessmen, doctors, politicians, but also drug dealers. The East was big houses and gated neighborhoods, where people came to escape the city's crime. We had a spot in a fancy complex with a pond called Frenchman's Wharf. One of my aunts helped us get the apartment, though we paid. It was 1980, and when I turned 12, I bought my first car, a 1979 light blue Cutlass Supreme. Driving isn't that hard, I thought, the wheel makes it go. Eventually I learned the pedals, long for fast, short to stop. I was still going to school, and each morning I'd get in my car, put in a cassette tape—Sugarhill, Run-D.M.C., Grandmaster Flash, Whodini, Kurtis Blow, LL Cool J—and get on the interstate.

Before school I stopped by the Projects. I exited at Louisa and took the back way down Poland to Florida. With the drug business, there is a flow, and 7 to 9 a.m. is busy. We hung in the same spots, the stairwells outside Lucky's place, and sold weed. Eventually we started selling powdered cocaine. You might ask, why would people buy drugs from kids? The answer was simple, we had the better product, and we gave people credit. I'd stay in the Projects until 8:15 or 8:20, then head to school, Andrew J. Bell, up on Ursuline in Treme, a historic neighborhood. Lucky went to Kohn Junior High in the 9th Ward. He had his own car, too, I think it was a 1970 Monte Carlo. Romeo stayed in the Projects. He never really was the school type.

At Bell I parked my car around the corner so no one would see me drive in. If anyone asked, I'd say a wealthy aunt got me the car. Bell was built in 1904, a big, beautiful brick building that looked like a fancy Catholic School. They had this one teacher named

Dr. Wilson, a strict, mean old lady who refused to retire. She taught English and was at Bell when my mother went to Bell. She had this old lady smell, and I don't know if she had arthritis or what, but one of her hands was like a claw. I hated that lady. When she called on me, she used my whole name, including my middle name, Daniel "Lannie" Bright the Third. I avoided her class all together and would go sit in Mr. Harris's class.

Mr. Harris taught history, and he taught history in his own way, realistic history, history from our standpoint. Our class was all black kids. Mr. Harris told us where we came from and what our race had been through. You go into a typical history class, and they have pictures of all these white guys up on the wall, the forefathers. Uh-uh, Mr. Harris didn't have that in his classroom. Someone once asked him, "Why don't you have any pictures of Abe Lincoln and George Washington?" Mr. Harris replied, "When these people were in power we weren't even considered human beings, so why would I have their pictures up in my classroom?"

Mr. Harris told us that most of what we call history is a lie. "Abe Lincoln didn't free you because he wanted to free the slaves, he freed you because he wanted to save the Union. If he could have saved the Union and kept slavery, he would have." Mr. Harris told us that the truth always lay within a lie, and it was our job to go between the lines, do our own research, find the truth, and change the way things were. If we didn't, we weren't going to last long, not in New Orleans anyhow.

"With all the drugs and killing going on in this city," said Mr. Harris. "You are an endangered species."

He knew guys sold drugs because they couldn't find jobs and had to help their families, and he knew he couldn't make them stop. He knew the older guys couldn't find jobs because they had been in prison. He knew what was really going on in the streets, and his way of helping was to get kids to come to school. If he looked out the window and saw someone shooting hooky, he'd say, "Hey, boy! Come sit in this class!" He would rather have you in his class than out there on the streets. I think he figured even if you were just sitting there, some knowledge might brush off on you. Each class you might have three or four kids in there who weren't his students, and I might be one of them.

Mr. Harris dressed nice, reptile shoes, silk shirts, Armani slacks, Gucci, Kenny Cole, the casual business player look. He had his silk shirt buttoned halfway up, his rings and his watch, and he wore a medallion. Being in Mr. Harris's class was when I really started wanting to dress nice. I peeped at his wardrobe and got tips. At first everyone thought Mr. Harris was gay, because of his clothes. But it turned out he was fooling with all the female teachers, and he was fooling with the female principal, too. If you looked good, he would get you. We had this algebra teacher, I can't remember her name, but I used to see her and Mr. Harris together after school. He had a Benz, brown or beige I think, and he'd drive her home.

At that time, I had a little mustache, earrings in my ears, and although everyone wore Adidas, I was wearing Gucci. I looked young, and yet I didn't look young. It was hard to tell just how old I was. I was ahead of my age. I came into class one day with some ostrich skin sandals and Mr. Harris just kept looking at me. I guess he was trying to see if they were imitation or real. After class, as everyone was leaving, Mr. Harris put his hand out and stopped me, "What you doing with these fancy type sandals on?"

I didn't say anything. I just smiled and kept walking. Mr. Harris had started putting things together.

"Dan, where do you get your slacks and shoes from?" he asked me one day. "They cost more than mine."

"Rubensteins," I said, meaning the big clothing store on Canal Street.

"How can you afford Rubensteins?"

Another time he saw me getting into my car, he shook his head and kept going.

"You just better know what you're doing," he later told me.

My mind was not on school. My mind was on the streets and women. Mr. Harris was also my role model for that. You have to remember, I'm coming from the Projects. The guys I know with a lot of woman are pimps. But Mr. Harris was the opposite. He was a player. He wasn't trying to degrade women. He was just trying to enjoy them. And by that time, I was trying to do the same.

When I was 11, Goldy told me, "It's time for you to have sex." He put me in a car and took me to an apartment in the East. There were three or four female roommates there, and Goldy was fooling with one of them. These weren't prostitutes. They were the type of women who fooled with guys making money, and Goldy was definitely making money. These ladies dressed nice, looked nice, had their own cars, and they knew that even though I was young, I was making money with Goldy. He went up to one woman, 26 or 27, brown eyes, light-skinned, what we call redboned, and said, "Show him what to do."

Her name was Val, and she took me into a bedroom and showed me what to do. It was like I was in school for sex. I remember when I first ejaculated I thought I was peeing in her. After that, whenever I could, I got one of the older gangsters to give me a ride over to Val's. And when I got my car, I drove myself, say on my lunch break at school. But mostly I went back to the Projects, because 12 to 2 p.m. was another busy time for making money.

They had a sandwich shop next to Bell, and at lunchtime all these little girls would come up to me: "Hey Poonie, buy me a sandwich, buy me a sandwich!" I'd buy like 20 sandwiches for these girls then walk around the block, jump in my car, and head back to the Projects to sell some cocaine. After school it was back to the Projects again. From 5 p.m. all the way up to midnight was another busy time. At night the Projects became like the beach in Miami. It was the best party you can imagine. Women waited until the sunset and came out with their little bitty shorts on, their hair down. Guys came out with their new Polo, their new cars. Everyone put on their finest outfits. And you had two or three clubs right there. These were neighborhood clubs, but they were nice-sized spots, with music and pool. Older people hung at Club Desire, or the Green Door, or Sunny's, but if you were in your 20s or 30s, or if you were kids like us who hung with an older crowd, you hung at 3J's. That was the hip spot. Everyone who had a little money, or looked like they had a little money, was there. And that's where all the women were at.

Back then drugs were not just a young man's game. Older men sold drugs, and even older women sold drugs, although they usually had a very specific clientele. Everyone was trying to survive, and drugs were just part of that. Coke was the big thing in the '80s. A lot of people used it for having a good time. Or, you dipped the coke, or joint, in embalming fluid, what we called *clickers*, because it clicked you out. Certain girls loved smoking that. Romeo would roll a bunch for the night and try to get girls high so he could fool with them. From the beginning, Romeo was diabolical.

After the clubs, we had our eating spots. Morrison's over in Gentilly, which was cafeteria-style. Or Anita's, on Tulane Ave and Galvez, which was soul food. Sometimes we drove back to the East, where there was a spot called We Never Close on Chef Menteur. Back then I was eating meat, so everything was ham and cheese on French, cheeseburger on French. The owners knew what we were up to, they knew we were a bunch of kids driving nice cars. At that hour, you're either coming from the club, or you're coming from the corner. But they didn't care, we were giving them business.

Even though I was still selling in the Projects, I wasn't going home. But my mother had ways of keeping track of me. She went out to the clubs and barrooms and talked to people. And by us having such a big family in the Projects, she kept tabs on me through them. "Have you seen him today?" she'd ask cousins and uncles. "Has Poonie been around?" She worried, and she prayed. If she heard gunshots in the Projects, she walked over to see if I wasn't lying face down in the streets. She missed me, but she knew she couldn't change me back into a little kid, and she didn't waste her time trying. As for my father, I didn't see him anymore, and he didn't know anything about my life. Goldy was becoming more and more like my father.

Goldy had a son named Little Goldy. He was about ten years old, and he was a badass kid. Goldy was a good father, but he used money and material things to make up for not being there. Little Goldy started to notice he could get anything he wanted. Goldy had a big place in the East, and other kids always wanted to come to Little Goldy's house because he had so many bikes and all kinds of video games and fancy toys. These kids asked Little Goldy a lot of questions, "What does your daddy do for a living? What does your mamma do?" As a result, Goldy didn't let him mingle much out there. But the East was also boring for Little Goldy. It was just a quiet upscale neighborhood. The real fun for a kid was back in the Projects. Goldy kept an apartment there, too, and Little Goldy got into a lot of mischief there. Breaking into abandon homes, stuff like that. He was trying to see how far he could push his parents.

Goldy's girl and Little Goldy's mama was a woman named Sandra. We called her Black Girl because she was so dark-skinned. Sandra was a tough lady. I wouldn't say arrogant but very confident. When she walked, she walked with a stride. All the women in the Projects envied her, and she knew that, she knew she had the man with the money. She was constantly going to the beauty parlor, getting her hair fixed. She had a nice house, Gucci dresses, the jewelry, rings on all her fingers, about ten necklaces around her neck, diamonds in her ears. Every time someone came in the Projects selling something hot, she would buy it, TVs, jewelry, clothes. The crooks knew exactly what size she was, and they would steal things just for her.

Sandra was a good mother. Her one fault was she liked partying. She'd get someone to babysit Little Goldy and hit every club in the city. During the day, she'd have friends over to their place in the Projects and let Little Goldy run about outside. One day he was out riding his little motorbike, and Sandra was inside entertaining girlfriends, drinking and smoking weed and listening to music. Suddenly someone came to the house and told Sandra that her son had just been hit by a car. She ran outside screaming. Everyone knew he was dead on the scene just by the way he looked. The bumper had hit him, and his mini bike had slid under the car. Little Goldy's head was split open. Sandra was devastated. Although I think she was more scared of what Goldy was going to do. His son had died on her watch. I forget where Goldy was, but he wasn't at home, and someone had to call him and tell him his son had just been killed.

Goldy was mad at everyone. He was mad at Sandra for not watching their son, he was mad at the guy driving the car for killing him, he was mad at people in the neighborhood for not keeping an eye, he was just lashing out. Goldy even said to me, "Where was you!?" And I was like, "Man, I was uptown." He was looking for someone to blame. For a little while, he blamed himself. He figured he should have been there. He should have been harder on him growing up.

Goldy wasn't much of a drinker, but after Little Goldy died, he drank a case of champagne and didn't leave the house for days. At fifteen years old, I had to take over the operation. I went to Baton Rouge to drop stuff off, I went to Houma, I went to Slidell. "Did you do this, did you do that," Goldy would ask me. And I'd tell him, "Don't worry about it, everything is alright." Goldy started to realize that I could run this organization, that I could do this on a bigger level, not just in the neighborhood but outside the city. In fact I was putting my personal touches on the business. For example the guy he dealt with in Slidell told me they had their shop going 24/7.

"No," I said. "We're gonna close at a certain time." The guy said that would cut down on profits.

"No, it won't," I said. "This way, people know when you close and make sure to get there on time."

So we tried that, and it worked. This also minimized face time. You're not out there in public at all hours of the day and night. It reduced our chance of getting caught. Plus you show respect to the authorities because you're shutting down at a certain time. I made them shut everything down on Sunday, too. You are living in a little bitty country town, you have to show some respect to these churches. On Sunday you have barbecues, old people come to town for services, kids go to baseball, DJs come outside with their music spinning records. People do a thing called splashes where they cut the fire hydrants and shut the streets. "If someone else wants to sell on Sunday, let them," I said, "as long as they don't sell in our area. It takes the heat off us."

First these guys looked at me like, "Who is this kid?" They were real skeptical. Later, when Goldy got back on his feet, they called him up and told him, "This kid is alright."

I hate to sound like I was waiting for Goldy's son to die because I wasn't, but once that happened, Goldy began spending even more attention on me. The conversation started changing. It was no longer just business. He took a real interest in my future. "What you wanna be in five years? Ten years?" Goldy asked me. "What are your long-term goals?" Goldy had loved his son, and when he passed, I guess I was next in line. He checked up on me at school, he came in to talk with my teachers. If I got in trouble and needed a parent to pick me up, he'd come. Some teachers thought Goldy was my father. And I called him father, and he called me son.

Goldy always said that even the drug business takes brains. He hadn't gone to college, and he didn't graduate high school, and I think that's why he pushed me so hard to stay in school. The top three high schools in New Orleans in the 1980s were John McDonogh, St.

Augustine, and Kennedy. I went to John Mac. That was the school to be at, like the Harvard of New Orleans high schools. John Mac had the best music classes, best sports, and it was the most popular. All the cool kids went there, including one of the most famous rappers of my time. Back then we had style. Big medallions around our necks and nice clothes, Guess and Polo, none of this pants falling off the ass shit. And nobody wore Nike, it was Adidas and Fila and All Star's. Goldy wanted me to graduate high school and go on to college. He was living his life through me. But I didn't want that life. I wanted the life he had introduced me to.

I was making $10,000 a week. My thinking was, you go to school to get educated to get a job to make money. But I already got money, so what I need the school for? I'm going to bypass all that and just make money. I had seen what money can do. I had seen how money could change people. The power it had. It changed the attitude of the people around you. Not that they feared you, but they respected you more. I wanted to be a millionaire before I was 30. I wanted to be one of the biggest and most powerful drug dealers in the city. I also wanted to be a legit businessman, like the guys in the Armani suits I had seen on Canal Street. I wanted to incorporate the streets into a corporate world. I saw myself wearing nice slacks and shoes and controlling a very powerful organization. I imagined pulling up to a fancy house, my 50-foot driveway, my wife in there cooking dinner, the kids playing in the yard. I get out of my car with my nice briefcase. At that time, that was my vision of a perfect life.

One night Goldy was at another woman's house, and her goal was to rob him. In the middle of the night, she unlocked the back door, and two guys came in. Goldy heard them and grabbed his gun. Then all the guns went off. When they stopped, one of the guys was dead, and the woman had been shot real bad. Goldy was wanted by the NOPD and went on the run. I was lying in bed one morning looking at the TV when the phone rang. It was Sandra. She told me that Goldy had gotten busted in Las Vegas, and they were bringing him back to New Orleans. When he got in, he called me from Orleans Parish Prison, what we call OPP. He said he wanted me to come see him.

Everyone in New Orleans knows OPP. Kids in New Orleans talk about prison the way other kids talk about college. "When I get up there I am going to do this and that…" As for me, every time someone talked about OPP I walked off. I didn't want to hear about that. I didn't want to go to no prison. Let's get some of this money and get out of here. That was my plan. But looking at Goldy, stuck in there for something that wasn't his fault, for defending himself, I began to realize that all the money and power he had didn't mean a thing now. The system doesn't care about that. When this system grabs you, they don't let go. That thought really shook me up.

"What do you need me to do?" I asked Goldy.

I was sitting in front of a small window, speaking to him through a phone. He told me what was going on and said it didn't look good for him.

"How much coke do you have left?" he asked.

He had been getting cocaine straight from a Colombian in Miami named Montana.

"Not that much," I said. "Four kis."

"Sell it," he said. "Then I'm going to hook you up with the Colombians."

He looked me in the eye and became real serious, "If you fuck this up, they will kill you."

That night at home, I sat back and thought, can I really do this? On the one hand, I was happy because I was the man now. Not second in command, but first. What I had always wanted. But I was worried that I wouldn't be able to handle the new responsibility. Then I realized, this was what I liked to do, and I already had a team, I had the platform setup, and I was good at it, it just came naturally. I got excited. I knew I could be bigger than I was. And I knew I could even be bigger than Goldy.

The next week I went back to OPP. Goldy gave me a phone number, and when I got home, I called the number. Some guy picked up. At first I didn't understand a word he was saying.

"Come see me in Miami," he said.

The trip was very important. I was practicing what I was going to say, how I was going to walk. I wanted this guy to respect me. I wanted him to see me not only as someone to deal with but someone to trust, someone who wouldn't break under pressure, someone who was young but could still run an organization and control the people around him. Goldy had been getting a lot of powdered cocaine from this guy, and it was my job to continue that relationship. I could easily have come away with nothing. Or come up dead. Was this guy even gonna want to do business with me? Or would he want to erase our history and move on with someone else? To do that, he'd have to erase me. All of this was on my mind.

Lucky and Romeo drove me to the airport. It was an early flight, and I sat in first class. There was this white lady across from me who kept looking nervously in my direction. Suddenly she asked, "Are you sitting in the right seat?"

I looked at her and said, in a very light whisper, "Bitch, my shoes cost $600, my socks cost $300, my shirt cost $150, my earrings costs $1,500, and this Rolex costs $5,000. So you tell me, am I sitting in the right fucking seat?"

She turned her head and looked out the window.

When the plane landed, a woman with long hair and pretty brown skin was waiting for me. She brought me to my hotel and in the afternoon returned and took me to a very big house, bigger than anything I had ever seen back in New Orleans.

Montana was a heavy-set older guy. If you didn't know he was a Colombian drug king, you'd look right through him and think he was just some old businessman. Montana spoke perfect English, but later I learned that when he got mad he talked fast, and his accent came on. He asked me to take a walk and toured me through the house.

There was a wall-to-wall saltwater fish tank, no sharks, but all types of colored fish, seahorses, and little baby octopus. There was a movie theater. Two marble staircases came up from the entranceway and met at the top. A conference room with TV monitors displayed the view from cameras placed around the house, and an elevator connected the conference room to the bedroom. Montana had a love for watches, and he had a walk-in closet strictly for his watches. He was also one of the first people I had seen with a bulletproof car, a big black Mercedes with beige interior. It had tinted windows and a phone.

The house was in a neighborhood of private beautiful homes spread around a lake. One home belonged to a member of the Miami Dolphins, this guy that snorted a lot of cocaine. Montana and I went out back and sat by the lake. There were kids paddling these little paddleboats around like bikes. Some were in canoes. Montana asked about Goldy. He wanted to make sure Goldy wasn't in need and that he had a good lawyer. But I told him that Goldy had his own money, he was alright. He stared out across the lake, thinking about something.

"Get your stuff from the hotel," Montana suddenly said. "You're moving in with me."

"Why?" I asked.

He told me that before he could give me anything, he wanted to get to know me. This was unexpected and shows how intelligent this guy was. My trip was well-rehearsed, and he knew that. He wanted to see how I reacted to things I hadn't rehearsed for. So I got my bags from the hotel, and for the next two weeks, I lived with Montana and his family.

He had a wife, two sons, and a daughter, the young lady who had picked me up at the airport. I'll call her Stacey. She was a prima donna. She got anything she wanted from her father. She had two or three cars, all the clothes, but she was also a nice person. Stacey wasn't a part of her father's world, but she loved her father a great deal, and she had to do certain things to help her family. When I first saw her at the airport, I thought, "I wanna hit that," but as time went on, I came to look at her as a sister.

I'd sit at the table and eat breakfast, and Montana would talk about the history of his people and how his family was fitting in here in the United States. There were two things Montana believed in more than anything: education and America. Everyone has a chance here, he said. If you educate yourself, you can do anything in America. Let's say you want to be an engineer. You train yourself in that field, and you go for it, and it can actually happen. Coming up in Colombia, Montana didn't have those luxuries, so he made sure his kids had them. He had achieved the American dream. Montana lived in a house with housekeepers and cooks. I don't even think he picked his own clothes. Whether it was his wife or a stylist, someone did that for him.

Mostly Montana did the talking, but occasionally he asked me questions. Why didn't I want to go to college? Why'd I choose this life? Was it forced on me or did I choose it on my own? I explained to Montana my reasoning, that there was no point in me going to college to get an education because you get an education to get a good job, and you get a good job to get a good paycheck. I bypassed that and went straight for the big check. He laughed.

"What are your views on the world?" Montana asked me.

"Everything on this planet revolves around two things," I told him. "Politics and money. I don't care what way you go, you cannot get around that. There will never be peace on this planet because as long as you have money and powerful men, they will always want power." That's the world I saw growing up in New Orleans, and that's what I told Montana.

He told me about his own experience in the world. He taught me things Goldy could never have taught me. He taught me world politics. He taught me about import, export, global trade. Montana was CEO of a lot of legitimate companies back in Colombia. He had a sugar factory, bananas, coffee beans, cocoa. If something was profitable in Colombia, in all of South America really, then Montana had some type of money invested in it. I started to see how these guys became kingpins. Colombia is a poor country, but it has all the wealth, the beaches, the harbors, the natural resources. I couldn't understand why this country was so poor until I realized that certain countries, including the United States, had embargos on these other countries. Even their neighbors couldn't trade with them. I started to see how different countries of the world were tied together through politics, and I started to understand how certain nations stayed on top, nations like the United States. These countries would do whatever they could to keep their power, to keep other countries from getting what they had.

Montana's brother still lived in Colombia and was part of the cartel. He made sure all the stuff got to Montana. A lot of people think they just fly the drugs over here, no. Montana had different professional routes, ships, trains, 18-wheelers, containers. From Colombia you had to go through other little countries, and each time you went through one of these little countries you'd lose maybe $5,000 or $10,000 that you had to give some local government official as a tax. America wasn't the only country these guys shipped to. They were shipping all over South America, and they were shipping to Europe, too.

Certain kids are ashamed of what their parents do, but at this time in Miami, everyone was involved in drugs in some form or fashion. Lawyers were linked to it because all their clients were drug dealers. Bankers were linked to it because the money in the banks was coming from drugs. Real estate developers were linked to it because the drug dealers were the ones buying up all the land and building big homes. The butlers, land-scapers, and gardeners were linked to it because they were getting paid to take care of these big pretty houses.

Even transactions that seemed innocent were really drug transactions. Say a lawyer had a client who was a drug dealer and went to buy a car. They're not buying that car, it's a drug dealer buying that car. They go to pay their kids' tuition, it's a drug dealer paying that tuition. They pay someone to cut their grass, it's a drug dealer cutting that grass. The city's whole economy survived off drugs. If it wasn't for drugs, Miami would have collapsed. You had guys walking into jewelry stores and buying 10 Rolex watches or going to Bentley dealerships and buying five cars at a time. Construction was going up all over the place. Everywhere you went you saw another building being built. The city was booming. And the whole cycle revolved around the drug trade.

Every city has a blueprint: New Orleans' was tourism and injustice. Miami was beaches and beautiful women. Daytime, everyone lounged around the beaches flexing their financial muscles. There were beautiful half-naked women of all colors on these beaches. At night was the club scene, everyone partying, snorting cocaine. Miami was also nice cars. The first thing I noticed in Miami as very different from New Orleans was the economy. For example, if I bought a Mercedes Benz in New Orleans at that time, I'd be standing out. But in Miami everywhere I turned I saw Lamborghinis, Rolls Royces, BMW, Mercedes-Benz, Jaguar, Ferraris.

At that time in Miami, there was a lot of land, a lot of trees and swamps. When I came back six months later, all that had been cleaned out and turned to condos. The real estate companies doing this were backed by drug dealers, and at the same time, many of the politicians and cops were crooked. Back then I'd say 50 percent of the politicians and cops in Miami were corrupt. I went into Montana's house one day, and a judge was in there having drinks with him. The whole system was rotten. On another occasion, I remember Montana was at a charity meeting, something having to do with saving the coral reefs. You have all types of environmentalists down there, and they'd buy these buses and take out the oil and motors, whatever else could pollute the water, then drop them onto the coral reef, so the fishes could have homes. And guess who was backing that coral reef project? Montana. I don't think Montana even knew what a coral reef was. That was all just to put him in good position with these politicians.

The one thing Montana took more seriously than anything was family. And most of all he cared about his daughter. Stacey was studying business at the University of Miami. She wanted to be a business-woman, educated and classy. And she had her own life, too. She went to friends' houses, she went to the beach. She partied and enjoyed herself, but she wasn't a wild type. Stacey was intelligent enough to know sneaking out of that house could be her death, so she wouldn't sneak out, not when I was there at least. Montana liked to keep the family close, to protect them, and during those two weeks, as I became more and more a part of that family, Montana started to have me do things for him.

Back in those days, the scene was dangerous. You had this Cocaine Cowboy thing going on between the Colombians and the Cubans. Shooting 100 bullets to hit one person, shooting in malls and on playgrounds. They even had a shootout in front of an elementary school. Bodyguards followed Stacey when she left the house, but Montana's men stuck out, they looked Colombian. Stacey's skin was black, and her eyes were green, she could pass for Cuban or black, and if Stacey was with me, people thought she was black. So Montana asked me to follow her and her friends when they went out to concerts and clubs.

I had to be on my guard. You had other kingpins trying to get on top, Colombians against Colombians. Then you had lowlife Cubans trying to kidnap people just for money. With the Cubans, you're talking a whole different breed. I don't know how to put this without insulting anyone, but the Cubans in Miami at that time were a real lawless group of individuals. They didn't care about the rules of business. They didn't have any code of ethics. And believe it or not, Colombians didn't like Cubans, and Cubans didn't like Colombians. They dealt with each other for business purposes, but that's it. I had to watch out for the jealous Colombians and the violent Cubans. It was a lot to keep track of.

One night one of Stacey's college girls got real drunk. We were at some warehouse that had been turned into a club. Miami does it like nobody else, they can take a barn and turn it into the hottest spot in the city, bubbles and foam and all that. Stacey knew all these spots, and against her pop's wishes, she went to them. This girlfriend of hers was on the dance floor, dancing wild, teasing the Cubans. "Time to go," I said and grabbed Stacey. I was going to leave her friend there. She wasn't my concern. But the Cubans followed us out of the club and came out holding onto the friend. Stacey tried to grab her. One thing led to another, and the Cubans surrounded me.

I pulled my gun out, grabbed one of the Cubans, and put it to his neck. "Get in the car!" I told the girls. I kept my gun on the Cubans, got in the car after the girls, and we left.

Other than that incident, we had a good time when we went out. And our plan worked, with me looking black everyone suspected Stacey was black, and no one bothered her.

Some time later, there was a war between different Colombian kingpins. Stacey wasn't allowed to leave the house. We snuck her out the back door just to bring her to college. I recall the one time I really saw Montana get mad, I mean really mad, was when Stacey disappeared. I was in New Orleans, and Montana called me at 3 in the morning,

"Get down here now!" he said. "Now!" He was speaking rapidly, and his accent was coming out. I could barely understand him.

"What's going on?" I asked him.

"No," he said. "Not on the phone."

So I got out of bed, paid like $1,000 for a ticket, and went. When I got there his whole family and everyone from his organization was there, trying to figure out what had happened to her. Some guys I knew, some guys I didn't. To get information, they were going to bring her friends in and torture them. But at like 4 or 5 in the morning, Stacey came sneaking back in the house. Turns out she had snuck out and gone to some big college party at a club in Fort Lauderdale. Montana went berserk, pitching stuff, hollering. I don't think Stacey had ever seen her father that mad. It was very, very stressful.

You have to realize, these guys had their own government, their own constitution, their own set of laws. That's what Goldy had always told me, and now I was seeing it for myself. Colombians were nothing to play with. Cross them and they're going to hurt you and your family. They act first and think second. With Italians family is off limits, but this wasn't the Italian mafia, this was the cartel. In the cartel, they don't give a shit, they hit everyone. The Colombians or the Cubans will put a hit on your whole family.

But that first time with Montana, I had a nice visit, and it was a successful business trip. Although I didn't know it then, I had a new family. I was 16. The average kid my age in America was preparing to go off to college or get some menial job, and I had just secured a connection with a Colombian drug kingpin to bring New Orleans quality cocaine. Most teenagers couldn't fathom doing the things I was doing, and especially no teenager out of the New Orleans Projects.

Chapter Four

King of the Projects

A few days after I returned from that first trip to Miami, two boxes arrived at my apartment. There were 30 kis in each box, at $15,000 a ki. After a few months, 30 turned to 40. We opened up shops. Then we opened up more shops. Shops were usually in somebody's house. We started getting other people to sell for us. At that time, my routine was get up and check the books, make sure my money was in order, see who owed me what, then go out and collect it. I dropped things back off, restocked, and checked to make sure everyone was staying out of trouble and not doing anything that would bring us attention.

Our customer base would surprise people. I had lawyers as clients, musicians, professional athletes, rappers. On the weekends, these people liked to party. When big people from out of town came for a game or concert, we hooked up with them. Afterward everyone went to the clubs, Rumors, Discovery, The Bottom Line, Club Nexus, Crystal's, Club Atlantis. We had graduated on from our little neighborhood clubs. These were high roller clubs. The clientele included drug dealers, ball players, entertainers, lawyers, bail bondsmen. No tennis shoes, no T-shirts. We wore Christian Dior suede sweat suits with some Gucci loafers. Lucky, Romeo and I had matching sweat suits in different colors.

They pat you down when you entered these clubs, so everyone left their guns on top of their tires. But some people got hip to that and walked around the parking lot taking all the guns. Then guys started hiding their guns under the hood, but I stopped doing that after the gun of some guy I knew went off and hit him in the shoulder. What happened is the gun had gotten hot, from being so close to the engine, and it misfired.

Lucky and them hit these clubs on a regular basis, but I only went every few months. Lucky liked the attention. He was always jumping into photos, but not me. I didn't like taking photos because I didn't like people to know who I was. Once someone knows what you look like, then they can spot you. You become vulnerable. When you're out like that, it's real easy for your enemies to find you. I was too focused on business to be spending time at these clubs.

I spent years watching the older guys in the Projects and watching the mistakes they made. I learned that in New Orleans, as long as there's no killing, you can make money. The New Orleans police only get involved when they have to, crimes against old people, crimes against kids, crimes that bring political attention or media attention. For powerful street-level organizations, war is bad. No one makes money, and both sides lose people. Plus you expose yourself to the federal government. My idea was always to come up with a solution where both sides could keep making money.

Say you try to move into my area and open a shop. We can't allow that to happen, but let's sit around and talk. Maybe we figure out that you're not selling what I'm selling. If you give me a little bit of your area, I'll give you a piece of my area, and we both benefit. If you don't like that solution, then give me 10 or 15 percent of your profit. There's always a way to negotiate. If someone in another part of the city was selling the same thing, then our plan was to bring them in with us, and we'd supply them. We had a better product, and we had no middlemen. Other people had to go through somebody to go through somebody to go through somebody. Thanks to Goldy's connection, our stuff was coming straight from the source.

At that time, we were making money, but our people were still suffering. I recall walking across the Projects and looking into one woman's house, I could look clean through to the other side because she didn't have any furniture. People were hurting. In wintertime or when school started, women lined up to tell us their kids didn't have nothing. "Okay," I said. "We'll take care of it." We got them clothes, we got them books. But I realized passing out gifts wasn't going to cut it. We had to do more.

The pool in the Projects had become a cesspool. The city had stopped maintaining it, and the water was green, and there were tadpoles and frogs in there. It looked like a canal. This was a nice-sized pool, maybe four feet deep in the shallow end and 12 feet in the deep end. We fixed it up, and the pool became a big scene. Kids swam in the morning and afternoon, but when the sun went down, the pool was for adults. It was like a fashion show, who had the best body, the best bathing suit, all of that. Most women didn't go in the pool. They just walked around the side. They didn't want to get their hair wet. Then you had the shelter house, where the changing rooms were at, and where most of the sex went down.

We did other things around the Projects. We put new swings up, merry-go-rounds, installed lights that went off at a certain time. We put in a football field, a basketball court. We made a real park. Everyone could come out and enjoy themselves. Kids could go for a swim, play ball, swing on the swings. Older women could sit on their stoops and gossip without worrying about getting shot. On weekends we brought DJs into the courtyard. And no one was allowed to sell drugs in this park. We called it the no-fly zone. We had a commission made up of the top people in our organization. If anyone got caught selling drugs in the no-fly zone, the commission held a vote to decide the penalty. Usually the person would be banned from selling drugs in our Projects. I witnessed some of the older gangsters sell drugs to pregnant women, but we never did that. I witnessed them sell drugs to kids, we never did that. The commission came up with laws, like our very own constitution. We took care of the neighborhood.

For kids age 12 to 15, we started a football league. Every Project had their own team, and some Projects had two or three teams. Football was an escape from reality, something to get kid's minds off the streets. But it was also a chance for people to flex their financial muscles. Most owners were drug dealers, and each owner was trying to outdo the other. We had nice uniforms with sneakers and helmets, coaches, assistant coaches, gyms. Practices were held in the park. Just like in a regular league, sometimes the games were home, and sometimes they were away games. We rented a van for the equipment and drove uptown, or across the river, to the Fischer Projects. These games were real big events. We would have a DJ spinning music, and everyone from the projects would come out to watch. Players on the winning team got a trophy, a gold chain with a football on it, and $100.

For the elderly folks, we gave them money for bingo. Every month we put addresses in a bag and picked two to get free rent. At Christmas we'd go somewhere like Kmart and buy 50 bikes. As we got stronger, we bought more: 100 bikes, 200 bikes. For Thanksgiving we got the elderly turkeys. One Mother's Day, we had a commission meeting and brainstormed. They had this little carnival in the Gentilly area, and me and Lucky went there and gave them $10,000 to come set up their entire operation. We had tables all around the park, food, rides, popcorn machines, merry-go-rounds, go-karts, the Dumbo elephant that goes up and down. We had this guy who owned horses come, and kids could ride around the park. Another area was nothing but games for adults. We made sure no one had to pay for anything.

Some people might wonder, how do you attend a fair sponsored by drug money? But our neighborhoods don't think like that. Our kids don't have many positive things, so anything fun that comes their way, they are going to accept. No kid's going to get off a ride because it was bought with drug money. Our plan was to build up our community, and whether it was with drug money or not, we were going to do it. People in our neighborhood had become accustomed to poverty. It's what they expected. They were used to the pool being broken, the basketball court being broken, the lights being broken, and them not being able to do anything about it. City Hall didn't fix these things. The Housing Authority didn't fix these things. We did. And because of that, people in the Projects respected us. It got to the point where I'd pull up in my car, and the kids would rush me. We became celebrities.

Our improvements attracted the politicians. One day I came into the neighborhood, and there were cameras and reporters there talking about the Projects being fixed up. The Housing Authority had a big press event, and they had taken the credit for all our work. Romeo wanted to rip it all down, but who are you hurting if you rip it down? "Let them take the credit," I said. Our people knew we did it, that's all that mattered. The government had failed them, and we became their government. But there was responsibility that came along with that. People got used to us, and they started expecting things of us. They depended on us for financial stability and also for security.

I recall one incident with a guy who beat his wife. I knew something was wrong because she never came the normal way to the store. She came the long way. She was always bruised up and didn't want anyone to see her. We asked her what happened, and she wouldn't talk, but everyone knew. One evening we caught her man coming home from work and told him that if he put his hand on her again, we'd inflict the exact same damage on him. Another time this guy came in the Projects and tried to grab a little girl. Her mama started hollering, and half the Projects chased him down and beat the crap out of this guy. With sticks, pipes, anything they could get their hands on. They whooped him half to death. When the police finally came, they threw him in the car and booked him. No one asked any questions.

The thing about cops and politicians is that they actually don't care if you're selling drugs, as long as you keep the violence to a minimum, the robbery and killing and raping. Even the cops know this city needs drugs to survive. If there are no drugs in New Orleans, no one is going to come here to party, and this city survives off the parties. So they have to keep the drugs flowing, but the police didn't like us showering money around the neighborhood like that, and they got back at us in their own way. We were a cash cow.

Anytime someone got murdered in the Projects, the 5th District cops picked us up and took us down to the station. The 5th District covers the entire 9th Ward, including the Florida and Desire Projects. Half the time, we wouldn't even know what the hell we had been arrested for until we had been booked. We never knew what happened, and a lot of the times, I don't think anything had happened, they just made it up. "You all committed a robbery," the cops would say. I'd be like, "Man, you know full well we didn't commit a robbery!" It was a setup, a nice little scheme so the police, the judge, and the bail bondsman could make some money.

What would happen is a trial date would be set, bail would be set, and we'd pay the bail bondsman. He'd give a cut to the judge, and later he'd also contribute to the judge's campaign. We'd get out on bail, and the trial would never go to court. When they needed more money, the police brought us back in. They ran this scheme time and again.

There were other things on my mind. One day I came into the projects, and there she was, sitting on the stoop with her girlfriends. Thelma was 21 years old, five years older than me. She had a college degree, a job, owned her own car, owned her own home. She had straight, clean, pretty white teeth, long silky hair, dark skin, and she dressed nice. She brought something to the table. She didn't have her hand out all the time. She was independent. The stuff I had and who I was didn't excite her, she had her own stuff and her own life. She was complete, and she was different than any other woman in the Projects. She was the woman I was looking for. Born in the Projects, she moved to New Orleans East, and when I met her was back in the Projects seeing some old friends. I got out of my car and asked a cousin of hers who she was.

"You don't recognize me?" said Thelma.

"No," I said. She was disappointed.

I asked her if she wanted to get a sno-ball.

"Why'd you want to get a sno-ball with someone you don't know?"

"You're one of those stuck up women, huh?" I said. "I ain't used to kissing ass, I'm used to getting what I want."

"That's your problem," she snapped back.

Eventually she decided to walk with me but was perfectly clear, "Don't think us getting this sno-ball means I'm going to have sex with you!"

After that we talked on the phone, and if we didn't talk, she came to the Projects to check up on me, to make sure nothing had happened. Most of the women in the Projects that I dealt with, I hate to say this, but their vocabulary wasn't too satisfying, it wasn't up-to-date. Thelma spoke well, she didn't curse. She didn't have tattoos. I didn't like women with these big tattoos all over their necks and legs. That wasn't classy. She had a good job at a nursing home, and she had other jobs, too. Most importantly I could trust Thelma. I didn't have to worry about going to sleep and not waking up or someone coming in the back door. I knew she wouldn't cross me.

Lucky and Romeo started seeing her around. "What are you doing getting serious with her?" they asked me.

I tried to play it off like the relationship with Thelma wasn't important. For a long time, I denied how much I really cared about her. But these guys were my best friends. They could see what was happening. As far as Romeo went, as long as she wasn't trying to hurt me or set me up, he was cool. And as far as Lucky went, as long as she didn't interfere with business, he was cool.

Thelma came from a good family, a classy and respectable working family. She had been married before, to someone in the gangster life, and he had been brutally murdered, shot up and stabbed. Thelma had always been attracted to that type. She had two kids, an 8-year-old girl named Ebony and a 5-year-old boy named Nick. Ebony was this little pretty black-haired girl. She was a real skinny kid and had long hair, all the way down to her butt. Me and Ebony got along. I'd come, and she'd be hiding behind the door, jump on my back, ask me to take her to the store. We went for little rides. If Thelma was gone, I'd cook the kids dinner. They loved creamed corn and white rice. Or we snuck out and went to Shoney's or Burger King. Thelma's girlfriends asked her, "You not scared to be around him?"

"Hell no," said Thelma.

"How you go to sleep at night?" one girl asked.

"I close my eyes and sleep," Thelma said.

Her family was tight. That confused me sometimes, and frustrated me, because her mother and brothers were always there. She was the only girl and had three brothers. Thelma's mother had a good heart, and she was street smart. She knew what I was doing because she had been married to an older gangster herself. Thelma's father had a real bad gambling problem, dice games. Not at casinos but these little gambling shacks and private gambling halls. You go there, and they buzz you in. He'd lose 30 grand then make it up then lose it again.

Thelma and her mother were best friends. They could talk about anything. Her brothers stayed with her mama, too, not because they couldn't get their own places, just because their family was so close. Eventually Thelma and I moved into a spot in the East together, and her mother moved there, too. I was trying to figure out how to get away from these people, and here they all come. Thelma sat me down and tried to tell me how it was, but I wasn't used to that. I'd come home, see them, and immediately want to get out of the house. But Ebony would be watching me leave. "Where you going, Dad?" I couldn't leave with that happening and would give her a nod, "Come on, let's go." We might go to the lakefront, or the park, get something to eat. Ebony loved taking a ride.

We became like a real family. Thelma came home after work and cooked dinner, though most of the time I couldn't make it. I'd come home from a day on the streets, and my food would be on the stove, and she'd be asleep. I'd take a shower and get in bed. If I had to stay out real late, if something came up, I'd call her to say I'd be late. I was living two lives, family life and street life. The family life was comfortable, it was stable, it was love, the life I wanted. But I wanted that other life, too.

CHAPTER FIVE

GETTING SHOT

Right next to Florida was Desire, and these two Projects couldn't have been more different. Desire was scraggly, slower, less advanced. It was like they were stuck in time. We had guns, and they were still fighting with sticks and razor blades. We wore Kenny Coles and Guess and Polo, they were wearing Lee jeans, Chuck Taylor shoes, and Youngbloods T-shirts. We drove cars, they were walking or taking the bus. We rolled in somewhere with three people, and if we needed more, we called them. Desire liked going places in packs, 30, 40, 50 guys. When you saw them coming, you knew they were Desire Projects people.

Area-wise, Desire was huge. Projects in Chicago and New York City had more people, but they went straight up. Desire had like 260 buildings, and each one was only two stories. The Projects was built on a swamp, and they didn't lay the foundations correctly, so these buildings were always sinking into the mud, gas and sewage lines breaking, people's porches falling off. The buildings were brick and sandwiched together, but inside was wood. You could knock a wall out and go clean through to the next building. When the police came, these guys just ran through the walls or cut a hole in the floor and dropped the drugs down— we couldn't do that in Florida because the walls and floors were made of concrete. Desire was a huge market, and we wanted a part.

Lucky was fooling with a Desire girl named Tweetie Bird, and Romeo was fooling with her friend, Fat Black, who was a big girl, 5'11 and all muscle. Tweetie Bird had a younger brother named Jo-Jo. He was doing his thing, selling mostly powdered cocaine, and he had a big name in that Project. He was always fighting and shooting, starting some shit. Jo-Jo was our in. One night Desire had a DJ outside, and Tweetie asked us to come. When we got to her house, Jo-Jo was there. He had Adidas with no shoestrings in them, rings on every finger, and about 100 chains around his neck. And these weren't little bitty chains. These were heavy metal chains.

Jo-Jo was too flamboyant, not the type of people I'm used to dealing with. You mark yourself when you dress like that. Nobody is ever going to forget you, including the police, your enemies, an eyewitness. Jo-Jo thought he was Mr. T or Slick Rick or something, and I was looking at Lucky like, "Who does this dude think he is?" Jo-Jo was young too, like 14, but he was big, he looked more like he was 30. He was supposed to have played football, but the streets called him.

We walked around the Projects with Jo-Jo, and everybody kissed his ass, like he was the head of the five families in New York. "Man," Lucky whispered in my ear, "we can make $5 to 10,000 a day in this big-ass project!" Lucky had always wanted Desire, and now was his chance. I looked at Romeo.

"I don't like these niggers over here," he said.

"Fuck liking them," said Lucky. "We want the money."

"You all just give me the shit," Jo-Jo said. "I will control all the niggers."

Lucky smiled. "Let's do it."

I had my doubts. I knew Jo-Jo was like Romeo, he liked putting that gun in his hand. How are you going to make money if you're at war all the time? But Jo-Jo was convinced he could control his people in the Projects, and Lucky was convinced he could control Jo-Jo, and I let Lucky convince me everything was going to be okay.

Before us Jo-Jo had been getting stuff from a guy uptown who owned some nightclubs and a record label. That guy was getting it from someone else, who was getting it from out of town. We were a better deal for Jo-Jo. Because there were less middlemen, we were cheaper, and our stuff was superior. As it turned out, Lucky was right. Desire was a jackpot. Just because it's the Projects doesn't mean there's no money flowing through. Where it was coming from, I have no idea, but there was a lot of money. Jo-Jo was making so much money in that Project we had to get help counting it. Shit was going too good. Something bad had to happen, and it did.

Thelma never liked Jo-Jo. "That wild motherfucker is going to get you in trouble," she said. I should have listened to her. But I was starting to drift away from Thelma in other ways. Tweetie Bird and Fat Black had another girlfriend, a slim dark-skinned girl named Liz, and they wanted me to get with her, though I didn't want to fool with her. But everyday these Desire girls came around, and one day I went by Lucky's house, and they were there.

"That little one likes you," said Lucky.

"Man, I just came here to give you this shit," I told him. "Where's Romeo?"

"In the room with Fat Black," said Lucky.

Out of the blue, it started raining. I didn't want to get wet, so I sat down to wait the rain out, and there she comes.

"What's up little one?" I said.

One thing led to another, and we had sex. A few days later, I flew to Miami to see Montana. I stayed out there for three weeks, enjoying the sun and the beaches. When I got back, I stopped by my mother's house, and Liz and her mother were there.

"What are you doing?" I asked.

"I need to talk to you," she said.

Her mother was looking at me with hate in her eyes. My mother was looking at me like, "Be cool."

"I'm listening," I said.

"I'm pregnant," she said.

"Pregnant!" What the fuck am I going to tell Thelma?

"What are you going to do?" her mother asked me. I didn't hear her, I was still thinking about Thelma.

My mother stepped in. "We are keeping it."

I looked at her.

"That's right," she said. "We're keeping it. I will raise the baby."

On my way home, I was happy and mad. I had a baby on the way, but it was the wrong mother. When I got to the house, Thelma was cooking.

"Are you hungry?" she asked me.

I didn't say anything. I just looked at her.

"What's wrong?" she said. She could see my expression, my body language.

"Come here and sit down," I said. And I told her.

She looked at me and started crying.

"What's her fucking name!?" she yelled. "What's her fucking name!?"

I told her everything.

"Are you fucking kidding me!?" she screamed. "Get out of my fucking house, get the fuck out before I go upstairs and get your gun and shoot you with it."

I wasn't going to let her hurt me, and I didn't want to hurt her any more than I already had, so I left and went to stay in a hotel—the best in New Orleans, $500 a night. When I went by the house to get my clothes, Thelma just looked at me and rolled her eyes. A few weeks later, I went to see the kids, and she asked where I was staying.

"Get your shit and come home," she said. "I'm going to forgive that baby but not that woman. How the fuck you let a young ho tap you like that?"

I just looked at her. I couldn't say anything because she was right. Several months later, Ronisha was born.

I would stop by my mother's house to play with her and leave my mom money. I had no more dealings with Liz, but that was a turning point in my relationship with Thelma. To her my daughter was conceived out of mistrust. It brought a new tension to our relationship. And I was still hanging out with Jo-Jo. That also made her mad.

One night we were all at a club with Jo-Jo. It was summertime, the music was jamming, and the women were half-naked. Personally I loved winter because it kept ordinary citizens indoors and the streets quiet and safe. In summertime everyone is outside, and everyone is fighting. Kids fight with sticks and knives over little trifles. Women fight over who has the shortest shorts on, or who slept around with whose man. Because everyone is outside, your enemies are outside too, and the violence starts.

At the club that night, some guy's woman was all over Jo-Jo. This guy got mad, and Jo-Jo started beefing with him. We found out he was from Uptown, but we didn't think much of it and left. A few weeks later, Lucky, Romeo, and I were in Jo-Jo's projects listening to a DJ spin in the courtyard. When you have a DJ out there, it's like a little baby Mardi Gras, hundreds of people listening to music and partying. The Desire Projects were so big that you had all these different ways in and out, which means you were very exposed. We didn't know it, but the guy Jo-Jo had gotten into it with at the club was watching.

After the DJ, we walked back to Lucky's car. The streets were real busy. I was never allowed to go first.

Romeo would always jump in front. But that night I was first. Suddenly a car drove by, and gunfire rang out, about 15 rounds. Everybody ducked, and then they all got up, except me. I had been hit seven times. Romeo and Jo-Jo ran off to shoot at the guys in the car. Lucky stood over me, and I looked up at him. Blood was coming out of my mouth.

"Don't move him!" someone shouted.

Lucky was in shock.

"Fuck that, Lucky, help me up," I said.

Romeo and Jo-Jo helped Lucky put me in the car. I remember having problems breathing. Shortness of breath. I made them crack the windows, so I could get more air. I was coughing up blood. They were doing maybe 60, fast but not fast enough, up Louisa Street to St. Claude and over to St. Claude General. I refused to close my eyes. I thought that if I closed them I would die, that I would never wake up.

St. Claude General is not a huge hospital. It's more like a little neighborhood medical clinic. The doctors and nurses were frightened because we came in with guns showing. I was in and out of consciousness, but I was aware of what was going on. It wasn't so much pain but anger. I was mad because I had allowed this to happen. I had let someone get that close up on me. The doctors hurried me into surgery. After that I don't remember anything.

Two days later, I woke up in a hospital bed at Charity Hospital. There were tubes everywhere. It must have been late at night because Thelma was in the chair next to me, sleeping.

"Hey," I called to her. "Hey."

At first she didn't hear me. Then she jumped up crying, "I told you to stay out of that Project!"

It was at the hospital that Thelma found out how old I was. When they took me out of the room for some test, she saw my charts. They brought me back in, and she shouted, "You're 16-years-old?!" She just kept saying that. "You're 16-years-old?!"

She walked out of the room, and as she did she passed my mother. "He's 16-years-old!"   My mom smiled.

"You are a lucky man," the nurse said when she looked at me.

I had been hit twice in the left arm, once in the stomach, twice in my leg, and twice in my right side. I had iron staples in my stomach to keep that wound shut. One of the bullets that hit my side hit inches from my heart, but the other was the most detrimental. It collapsed my lung. Doctors put these pipes in there, tubes to inflate my lung back up. To this day, it's a little numb. They waited a few years to take the bullet in my chest out. The bullet that hit my leg exited under the back of my left buttocks. They told me I'd have a problem walking for the rest of my life.

Thelma hung around. She had gotten over my age, and my mother asked her to help tend my wounds. On the one in my stomach, the staples went all the way down to my private area, and my mama was not going to deal with that. I was in pain, but they had me on morphine. Thelma would start in telling me how I shouldn't have been hanging out with Jo-Jo, and I'd be like, "Shot time!" and hit the buzzer for more morphine. The doctor would come, and I'd say, "Yo, I'm in pain, Doc."

"You're not in pain," Thelma would say, "you just don't want to talk."

"I'm going to talk to you in a couple hours," I'd say, then drift off, and when I woke up again, I'd say, "I'm in pain again, Doc!"

Females from all over the city were trying to see me, but Thelma wasn't having that. "What do you want!?" she snapped at them. Thelma gave the hospital names of who could visit me and who couldn't, my immediate family, Romeo, Lucky—that was it. When Romeo came, you could see the guns on him, the bulge. He didn't care, and the nurses never said anything.

The sad thing is they didn't let Thelma's kids in. She told them I had fallen off my motorbike, and they wanted to come see me in the hospital. "Call home," Thelma said. "Talk to Ebony and Nick." But I didn't want to talk.

When they realized who I was, the guys who had done the shooting had skipped town. I was still trying to piece this thing together. I called Montana and told him what had happened.

"Do you need me to come down there?" he asked.

"No, I'm alright," I said. "I'll see you in a few weeks."

The hospital let me go home under the condition that I stay on bed rest. I was still living in the East, and Lucky stationed like eight guys around my house, just to be safe. He took care of everything he normally took care of, plus everything that I normally took care of, except for dealing with Montana. I couldn't allow that to happen. I sat inside for a month, getting my strength back. I had lost a lot of weight. In the morning when I tried to move, I had pain, but they had given me all these pain pills. Half the time my mind was in a fog. Eventually I started moving around alright. I realized that I was in a major business and before the shooting I hadn't been taking it 100 percent. After I got my health back, I tried to take the business side of things more seriously. Because of that, Thelma and I drifted apart.

But with the Projects being the way Projects are, it was hard to focus. I had become a legend and getting shot only made me more famous.

CHAPTER SIX

IN LOVE WITH TWO WOMEN

The Projects had some really nice looking women, women you could put on the runway in Hollywood or Paris. Some women used their looks to dance and strip. Some used their looks to attract men and money. Some used it for the right reasons. For example they might dance to make money, so they could go to school. Some used their looks to hook an athlete, or entertainer, or a drug dealer. Women wanted to have a baby with people like me. It was a badge of honor. That gave them power and protection. In the inner city, shy pretty females get jumped, but that won't happen if people know they have a kid with a powerful street personality. Women would stop by my house when I wasn't around. I'd come home, and they'd just be lying in my bed.

"What are you doing?" I'd ask.

"Waiting for you."

Women were taking pictures of themselves in their drawers and bras and putting the photos under my windshield wipers. I'd be driving, and women would be sitting on me buck naked. At night we'd go to the lake, beautiful women in bathing suits, or no bathing suits. At our clubhouse, Romeo and I would stand next to each other and see who could have the most oral sex performed on them. And 15 or 20 women would line up. They weren't ashamed. It was a competition for them, too. They were trying to show us who could do it better. And these weren't crackheads. These were gorgeous women.

Go to Romeo's house, and he might have three or four women living there with him, and they'd be walking around in their underclothes. Threesomes, foursomes. But that threesome thing every man wants is overrated. Each woman wants their time, so you have to make sure you please both of them. You have to spend time with one then go back to the other then go back again. If you are only entertaining one, the other will push her out of the way. Or they start paying attention to themselves. Although back then, it wasn't as common for women to lick on each other.

I liked square women, like Thelma, but there was one woman I fell in love with from the streets and that was Shelita. She was a big, fine, curvy redbone with short hair and a sexy smile. No tattoos, just a clean-cut pretty street female. You had to fall for Shelita, just her attitude, her aura. She had this Bonnie and Clyde thing, a ride-or-die chick. She was solid, no fat, just toned-up, muscular. You knew her from the way she walked. I could spot her from two blocks away. She strutted like she was on a runway. She might be walking toward the car. "How long you gonna be till you get here?" I'd ask, smiling. Shelita demanded attention.

She had grown up in the Florida Projects, but I didn't know her. I can remember this little girl smiling at me. She had a crush. Time went on, and no one was watching, but she was growing. She was becoming a beautiful woman, and when she realized she had this beautiful body, she came back around and said, "Remember me?"

I asked about her, and someone told me she was a hustler. Growing up I think she worked at a fast food restaurant, Popeye's or something. Shelita had a big family, maybe four brothers and one sister, and she took care of them. By the time she bought school supplies and clothes, she was broke, so she started selling drugs. And she really blossomed. She started off by herself but eventually had three or four girlfriends dealing for her. She had her own little crew, and her own clientele. They were not on a major level yet, but they sold, and as time went on, Shelita got bigger and bigger.

"Put her on the team," I told Lucky. And we did. At first I was looking at her out of sex eyes. If you're a part of that life, you are going to fall for Shelita sooner or later because she has your back. If I told her, "We're going to jump off this building together," she'd say, "No, this building isn't tall enough, let's jump off a higher one." Not only that, she's going to sell as much drugs as you do. I recall Shelita being pregnant and still hustling. Most of the time, she wore jeans and tennis shoes, comfortable clothing for someone out on the streets all day hustling. Shelita started coming to our commission meetings. One day Lucky did most of the talking, and afterward she came up to me, "Who am I taking orders from, you or him?"

"Who you wanna be taking orders from?" I asked her.

"You," she said. That was the start of our relationship.

Shelita was also one of three or four females in the Projects who could really fight. She didn't just pull hair and scratch. Shelita fought like a man. I've seen her belt women in the mouth just for looking at me. She'd wait until I was gone then go up to the girl and punch her. People knew not to mess with her. I remember I had been fooling with one of my sister's friends, this girl named Tory, and she really didn't like Shelita. Tory got a doctor's scalpel and said she was going to cut her.

"You better know what you're doing," I said, "because Shelita will beat the shit out of you."

Tory didn't listen, and she came up to Shelita on the street with this scalpel, "I'm going to cut your throat!"

Shelita kept a small little gun in her purse, and she pulled it out, "I'm gonna shoot you right in your fucking leg!" Tory turned and walked off, and that was the end of that.

Other times I recall guys coming in the Projects and shooting at Romeo. Shelita would start shooting back.

"What you shooting for!?" I'd say.

"They shouldn't be coming in on our set!" she'd reply.

But Shelita was a good person. Anytime someone was in need, she'd give them money. She had two kids from before me, and she took care of her mother and brothers and sisters, too. One of her sisters was working and going to school, but she had a baby brother named Money who was following in her footsteps. He was 12 years old and selling coke for her. Money had all the potential to be in the real hustle. He was obsessed with gold and putting gold teeth in his mouth, that was the thing back then. After a while, all of Shelita's siblings except her oldest brother got into the business. Mostly she gave them drugs to sell, so they stopped asking her for money. She'd give them each like $300 worth of stuff and tell them to keep $200 and bring her back $100. She was trying to teach them to be responsible. Shelita was the big sister, and they were family, her brothers and sisters looked up to her and respected her. They all lived together in an apartment on Congress Street.

Around that time, my little brother started doing wild shit. He had his own little crew, and they did petty things, holding people up, snatching purses, robbing drug dealers, pistol-whipping people, dumping guys out of wheelchairs. He wanted to be like me, he wanted to get a reputation for being a tough guy. But he was going about it the wrong way. He was causing himself unnecessary attention, and that wasn't going to fly with us. One day he jumped a guy in a wheelchair just for looking at his girlfriend. When I confronted him about it, he said the guy had grabbed her. He always had a reason. I tried to help him out by giving him little jobs, but whenever I gave him something, he messed it up. My brother never fooled with drugs, and he didn't drink, but he was always short on money. I had set him up with a guy we used to call Pretty, and I asked him, "Pretty, what's he doing with all his money?"

"Man, he's got a strip club habit," said Pretty.

I'm talking thousands of dollars at the strip club. And not just one strip club, every strip club. New Orleans East, French Quarter, across the river. Every night he'd go to a different strip club and give his money away. And he was still misbehaving on the street. Eventually all these evil little crimes caught up with him, and he spent some time at OPP. When he came home from prison, we gave him a big party at the Holiday Inn in the French Quarter. My little sister was there, and Shelita was there, too. We were all drinking Dom Pérignon and having fun, and then Tyra came. When I saw Tyra, I almost dropped my glass.

At that time, my sister was growing up, and she was developing her own style and her own life. I would meet her in the Projects and give her money. Whatever the current style was she wanted it, she was always in need. "I seen these shoes," she'd tell me, "I seen these jeans." She asked me for things my parents couldn't afford. I think me being who I was became somewhat of a curse. Guys didn't talk to her because they were scared I'd get mad, so she had a hard time finding boyfriends. She was about three inches taller than me. When she was 16 or 17, she moved out of the house. Just like me, she wanted her independence. She worked at a fast food restaurant and moved into an apartment with her girlfriends, and Tyra was one of her roommates.

Tyra had two sisters and four brothers, but she was the baby of the family and the favorite. Being the baby, Tyra stayed home and took care of her mother, who was very controlling. The other sons and daughters didn't want to be around the mother, so when they could, they left. Eventually all of Tyra's brothers were killed, one after another. One was gunned down in the streets. With another a girl let somebody in on him while he was sleeping—same thing that happened to Goldy—and she shot him in the head for the insurance money. Another son died playing Russian Roulette, he blew his own brains out. The last to be killed was Lou. He was the youngest, and him and Tyra were real tight.

Because of what had happened to her brothers, Tyra developed this meanness. Then, one of her sisters got AIDS from her partner and died pretty quickly. After that Tyra was responsible for raising the two nieces her sister had left behind. She was also going to school at Southern University at New Orleans. I think she wanted to be an English teacher. She wanted to do something with her life. I was attracted to that. And she could survive on her own, she had learned that growing up, watching her brothers and sisters die, and taking care of everyone.

That night at my brother's party, Tyra had on some Jordache jeans and a brown shirt. She was beautiful. I pulled my sister aside, "Who is your girl?"

"Tyra," she said. "She doesn't fool with your kind."

"What's my kind?"

"She only fools with square dudes."

"Yeah, we'll see about that."

Later that night, I sent Tyra a bottle of champagne. She sent it back.

The next day, I met my sister in the Projects, and there she was. "Get out of here!" I told her.

"Fuck you," she said. She and my sister went to leave.

"I'm just playing with you," I called after her. "Why you so mean?"

She rolled her eyes. Tyra drove a sky blue Cavalier, and she was halfway to the car. I ran behind her. "Let me walk with you."

"Don't you have enough women," she said.

"No, I don't have any women."

"Boy, your name is hotter than the sun."

"Is that right?"

"Yeah, that's right," she said.

When she unlocked the door, I jumped in.

"Get out of my car," she said.

"No, not until you talk to me."

"Come on and get out. I have to go get my mother something to eat."

"I'm coming," I said.

"Okay," Tyra said. "But you are buying the food."

I looked at her. "I can do that."

My little sister got in the back, and I got in the front.

"Why don't you like me?" I asked Tyra.

"First of all, you sell drugs. And you have too many women. And that girl you fool with, I don't like her."

"What girl?" I asked.

"Shelita, that's who."

"Shelita is my business partner," I said.

Tyra just looked at me.

"I did my homework on you, too," I said. "All your brothers were drug dealers."

"Yeah and they're all dead and that's why I don't fool with drug dealers!"

For the next few days, Tyra and I spoke on the phone. One night she let me take her to the movies and dinner.

"What do you want me to do now?" I asked her afterward. "Do you want me to bring you home?"

"I don't care," she said. "Whatever you want to do."

We stopped at the liquor shop and got two liquors. I pulled into the parking lot of a very nice hotel.

"Am I setting myself up to get hurt?" she asked.

"I will never hurt you," I said.

Some people say you can't be in love with two women at the same time. I totally disagree. These women can be very different, and you're in love with their differences. One part of you wants the dangerous woman, who is part of your dangerous lifestyle. The other part of you wants the square woman, who is part of that safe family world. Tyra and I used to play football, basketball, videogames, that was our connection. Shelita and I used to bag up drugs, sell drugs, and watch out for each other on the street, that was our connection. But the relaxed world I had with Tyra couldn't have been possible without the street world I had with Shelita. Tyra hated on Shelita, and I'd tell her, "Where do you think all the money comes from? That house you sleep in? That car you drive? Shelita is making that money, she's out on the streets every day busting her ass."

Shelita was the material type. She spent $1,000 on an outfit, got the shoes, her nails done, her hair done. Tyra wasn't like that. I tried to get Tyra a Lexus, she didn't want it. "I don't need that kind of car," she said. We went to the Gucci shop in the mall on Canal Street, and I tried to buy her Gucci dresses, Gucci shoes. She didn't want any of that. One year for the Essence Festival, I gave her $3,000 to get something to wear.

"You gonna spend all this money on one outfit?" she asked me.

"That's what this thing is all about," I said.

She went into Payless and got a whole trunk of stuff. "I ain't gonna spend all this money on one thing," she said. "I'm gonna get a bunch of clothes and have enough to pay my bills afterward."

She was right all along. She knew there were other things to do with money. And besides, she still looked good with her clothes from Payless. Tyra used to wear these beige pants, I don't know if she painted these pants on or what. If she was mad at me or wanted something, she just put those pants on.

And then Shelita got pregnant. Tyra was supposed to be taking the pill, but when she found out Shelita was pregnant, she stopped, and four months later, she was pregnant, too. Her mother was furious. For a long time, she had controlled Tyra like a robot. And she really didn't like me because I was taking her last surviving child away from her. But I didn't care. I was in love with her daughter.

Shelita gave birth to twins, Dana and Daniella. Dana's nickname was Peanut because she was skinny with a round head like a peanut, and she was always crying. Daniella was like a fat little bubble, and so we called her Bubble. She was real quiet and never said anything, she just observed. When Tyra was in the hospital giving birth to my son, it was Shelita's birthday. She was throwing a party at this club called Whispers. I went to the hospital then snuck off to Whispers, came back and watched my son come into the world, then went back to the club. Back and forth, back and forth. Luckily both spots were in the East. Still it was a sign of things to come. It was too stressful to be involved with both of these women.

My mother and I still weren't seeing each other that much, but my kids became a brace for us. Shelita was so busy running around taking care of business that she didn't have time for the twins, so she asked my mother to help. Now my mother was raising the twins and Ronisha. There are mothers that can't even handle themselves, and there are mothers who are always taking in children. My mother was in the second group. And the women knew what type of mother I had as far as Project mothers go. My mother was the oldest of seven kids, three brothers and four sisters. She had to help raise them, take them to school, feed them before she fed herself. My mother had been raising kids her whole life. I think if she didn't have little kids to help raise in this life, my mom would have passed long ago.

But it bothered me that I wasn't around much for my kids. I was getting burnt out. Things were starting to fall apart. And the streets were getting more dangerous. The idea of getting out was in my head. Tyra was always trying to tell me how to get out. And Shelita was always saying, "Fuck getting out, this is our game."

CHAPTER SEVEN

HUSTLERS AND ADDICTS

If you buy a large amount of drugs in New Orleans, it is probably going to be trash. Most city drug dealers don't like traveling, so they'd rather deal with middle-men and pay big prices for an inferior product. We were always traveling, and before 9/11 everything was easy. We brought drugs in with U-Hauls, if police didn't have a tip, they didn't fool with the truck. Or we caught a train, that was also easy back then. Or a bus. We chartered Greyhounds to Pensacola or Miami or Disney World. I might get my aunt to throw the trip, and everyone would buy a bus ticket. Meanwhile that trip is just camouflage for us to get the stuff in. The only ones who knew about the drugs were me, Lucky, and Romeo. Everyone else thought they were just going to the beach.

Picking up drugs was routine. In the movies, you see guys standing around with their guns testing it, then all the guns go off. It wasn't like that. But there were rules, and rule number one was nobody kept drugs at their house. Even I never knew where the stuff was. Montana would tell me to go to a certain place, and it would be there waiting. My job was to hand over the money, and get the drugs back to the city. People using drugs, and even your average guy on the corner selling drugs, had no idea where these drugs were coming from. And they didn't care either. They just wanted that high.

In the mid-1980s, we got some heroin in and didn't know how to cut it, so we left it pure and put that poison out. People from all over the city came to our Project looking for this dope. We were more than satisfied with the cocaine, but with heroin our business went to another level. We were selling maybe $10,000 worth of heroin a day, in $25 bags, from 6 in the morning until 7 at night. We didn't even count the one-dollar bills because there were too many. We gave them away to kids. I had money stashed so many places. Money stuffed under the sun visor of different cars I kept around the city. Money buried in this yard and that yard. I put money in the sheetrock, the bottom of the ice box, the bottom of the washing machine. I opened my jacket pocket one day and found $30,000. There are only so many places you can hide money.

When you're dealing drugs on that level, you come in contact with all sorts of crazy people. I had ex-military guys bringing me guns and bulletproof vests. I had six or seven bulletproof vests. I had a 1986 bulletproof Mercedes Benz—I got the idea from Montana.

Growing up in the Projects, everyone was fixing cars, so I knew a lot of mechanics. One guy told me he could bulletproof my car, no problem. Just reinforce the top of the doors, the trunk, and around the fenders. Then you need steel shocks to hold the extra weight. Montana told me of a place in Miami to get the windows done. I barely drove that car, maybe to a big concert like Jazz Fest, and I don't think I really needed it. I wanted it because I could afford it. We were trying to figure out what to do with all the money, and most of the time, we were just wasting it. Fast money goes fast because you figure you can always get it again.

When we got that heroin, it was like the whole city stopped going where they were going and started coming to us. Doesn't matter what part of the city you're in, if you have good heroin, people will talk, they'll want to know where someone got it and how they can get it for themselves. Good heroin sells itself. You don't have to campaign. Consumers in the drug business are messed up. The more powerful the drug, the more they want that drug. Say you have heroin that people are ODing on. Users aren't going to be running from it, they're going to be running right at it.

Everything hit the fan. There were too many people. We had this new line of customers, which meant we were stopping other people from making money, because their customers were coming to us. Now we had enemies in the 17th Ward, we had enemies across the river, we had enemies uptown. Lucky or I occasionally sent people to buy drugs from someone else, just to see how big their bags were, or how good their stuff was. That way we knew what the competition was pushing out, and we had to do better. But we always had the advantage. Our drugs were coming straight from the source. We had fewer middlemen, and our supply was more pure.

Heroin had always been around, but it was never huge. When we started selling, that changed. One day I walked through the Projects and saw everyone in this trance. People were nodding off like they were half-asleep, walking around in a daze, scratching. Heroin is a downer, and if it's some real good dope, you might go into a duck—what some people call nodding out—and wake up 20 minutes later, or an hour later. In the street life, that's a bad thing because you need to be watching your back.

The heroin took over, but the coke scene was still good. Then about 1988 our powder profits started slipping. We were wondering what the hell was going on, why things were slowing up. It was crack. When it first came on the scene, I didn't really want to cross over. I was good with the powdered cocaine and heroin. I thought, man that will never happen, crack will never be big like cocaine. I was wrong. Crack spread like wildfire. It started in the Desire projects. Everyone was making all this money on it, and everyone wanted to do it.

"I don't want to be cooking and selling that," I told Lucky and Romeo. But Lucky wanted to try, and he started making a lot of money. Okay, I thought, our game has changed. We need to do this because if people don't get the crack from us, they're going to get it from someone else. If guys in the Desire projects were selling crack and making money, we had to be selling crack. First we had to learn how to cook the cocaine up. We had to transform it from powder to rock. I knew a female who used to freebase, so we called her up, and she showed us how to do it, but she did it on a small scale. We needed someone to show us how to do it on a larger scale, a kilo at a time, so we found this guy in the Iberville projects named Snow.

Snow was a big guy, like 6'5. He used to play basketball, but I think he hurt himself, and somehow he became real good at cooking up crack. Lucky learned from Snow. Lucky was the type of guy who could watch something and catch on quick. He found out what temperature was needed, how many times we had to stir it around, he got the whole process down. Making crack is not that hard. All you need is powdered cocaine, baking soda, and some real hot water. Put water and baking soda on the coke, put some heat on it, rock it up. That's it.

When the crack hit, everything went downhill. People started selling stuff out of their houses, selling their kids' toys, selling their families' food stamps, women selling their bodies. With crack you lose your dignity, your pride, your self-esteem, your ego, your goals, your visions. You lose yourself. You don't take care of your hygiene. You wear the same clothes. Hustlers like Shelita wear the same clothes because they're active out there on the streets and need a comfortable outfit, but you can tell the difference between a hustler who is wearing the same clothes and a crackhead who is wearing the same clothes. Crack separated the hustlers from the addicts.

Nice females started smoking crack, and they stopped coming outside. I would see them in hallways on their knees, doing things for crack. One female I was dealing with, this beautiful college woman named Tanya, dropped out and started hanging around another Project. I went to see a guy I knew over there, and he told me they had a pretty little girl turning tricks. I saw this girl coming out of the hallway with someone. It was Tanya. She saw me and put her head down and kept on walking. I didn't want to see her, and she didn't want to see me, not in that state. I saw girls I had gone to school with, girls with jobs, college girls, all smoking crack.

I used to know teachers and docs using heroin. I used to know teachers and docs smoking crack. You can tell the difference. With heroin a lot of people don't even know you're using. You're still dressing nice, getting your hair cut. Especially if you have money, you don't go through the whole transformation. Even the broke older guys shooting up kept long sleeve shirts on to cover their tracks, and they had nice long sleeve shirts. With heroin you can get a bag, snort it or shoot it and go on into school, go to work. It's still possible to function in the world. And if it's good heroin, you don't need that much, a $25 bag will hold you all day. You might not even do the whole bag, you can hold half until later. Some guys might buy five bags, and you won't see them for the rest of the week.

With crack there's no limit, you can spend $300 or $400 in a day. You'll see the person using and then using again in another hour, not even another hour, another 30 minutes. You can never get enough. People stop being the people they once were, all they care about is getting more crack. And crack doesn't discriminate. It hits everybody. Once you get on it, I don't care how much money you have, you might think you can maintain, but you can't. When that money runs out, you are going to degrade yourself to get more crack. Someone trying to get crack will stop at nothing. I mean, nothing. When it comes to crack, nothing should surprise you.

Crack is especially bad for women. Women sell their bodies, sell their baby's toys, their baby's clothes, sell the TV out of their houses, perform oral sex in the hallway, in the street. When real pretty women get on drugs, men mess with them. "You were all high on yourself before, now get on your knees and do this for some crack." A man can always bounce back, he can change. Black men are expected to recover, you fall but you get back up. For women, it's harder to get your image back. Even if that woman changes and straightens her life out, she gets an education and gets a job, some man will come along wanting something, and she will say no, and he will say, "You were doing it when you were on that crack." The only way a woman can get that respect back is to leave and go to another state.

When the crack hit, Romeo's horns came up. One day I came into one of our shops, and Romeo had a woman sucking a dog's dick for crack. I just looked at him and shook my head. How could he even come up with something like that? The thing is, and this may sound crazy, but that wasn't a big deal coming up in the Projects. By the time you are a little kid, you have already seen so many things that there's almost nothing that will surprise you anymore. People abusing their own bodies, people abusing other people's bodies, people abusing animals. You know what all of this looks like, and you are numb to it. It becomes normalized. Sucking someone's dick for crack, or letting three or four people go up in them in a hallway, all that is normal in the Projects. And sucking a dog's dick for crack, that might not be normal, but you've seen enough versions of that, bits and pieces, and so it becomes like it is normal.

I don't know that Romeo had a psychological disorder. I think it was more egotripping and power-tripping. Romeo is what he is, I can't dissect it any more than that. And I definitely couldn't change him. Romeo would take that crack and do anything he wanted to people. You might come in the shop, and he'd have three women in the bed with him. Even though he was doing that before, it was different now. These were different types of women. They weren't doing it for fun. It was for drugs. Romeo made these women do things for crack, eat on each other, urinate on each other.

Even if you weren't on crack, it affected you in some way. Maybe your daughter was on it, or your son was on it, and they were stealing from you. It's sad when a mother can't put a purse down in her own house, when she has to inventory anything of value to know whether her kids have stolen it or not. Crack was literally ripping families apart. Square women who took good care of their kids might come around. "What she doing on it?" we would say. You had kids going to school with ragged shoes, or with no shoes, because mama sold the clothes to buy crack. Kids came around to us, crying, because mama took their bike to buy crack. We would replace the bike, we would get people food, pay their rent. But the more we tried to help people, the faster they fell apart.

One of my aunties got on crack bad. It got to the point where she was doing all kinds of stuff to get it, selling herself, performing oral sex. I knew she had to be getting it from one of my people. I didn't want to see her doing these things to get crack, but I knew I couldn't get her to quit. It was a dilemma. In the end, I told my guys, "Just give it to her for free."

A few people could use crack occasionally and be okay. I knew one heavy-set female, a nice looking young lady who used crack to lose weight. She might smoke crack for four days straight, and then the next week, she wouldn't fool with it. She sold it, too. She had a nice car, and she dressed nice. You could never tell if she was using or not. But most people weren't like that. Most people couldn't function normally once they got hooked. And you couldn't tell them to stop. Telling a crack user not to use isn't an option because they want that feeling so bad, they want that high. What a lot of people don't realize about crack is once you get that first hit, it's all you want. You are running behind that first hit, you'll always be looking for it, but you'll never find it because you've already had it.

The only way you can stop using drugs is if you want to stop. You can go to rehab, you can go to prison, you can spend all this money doing all this shit, but if you don't want to stop, you're not going to stop. You have to be willing to say, I've had enough. And you can, I've witnessed people do it, but that's not the majority. The majority of people crumple. When we first started out, the Projects was like family, people were out there playing football, volleyball, softball, females out on the stoops having fun, grass was cut, things got done. When crack hit, the neighborhood fell apart, and the whole city changed. It was devastating. Crack was the single worst thing ever to hit this country.

The crime rate jumped up, the murder rate jumped, the robbery rate, the carjacking rate, kidnappings. And we were now at risk, too. People knew the consequences if they crossed us, but when the crack hit, they didn't care. Everyone knew Lucky's car, and no one ever messed with it, but after crack hit, his car got robbed. I started wearing a bulletproof vest because now the same people who wouldn't dare try to challenge me before were on this crack. They didn't care anymore, and I had to protect myself. The whole scene changed.

Crack was everywhere, and I was pushing it everywhere. I take blame for it. I knew it was wrong, and I was a part of it. But what could we do? Stop selling. We stop selling, other people start pushing. If they're not buying from us, they're buying from our enemies.

I felt bad for the drug consumers, though no one was forcing them to buy these drugs from us. People have free will. If someone told me they were trying to quit, I backed off. "Stick with it," I'd say. We sold to adults, and adults have their own minds. We never sold drugs to kids or pregnant women, that was part of our constitution. But Romeo had started breaking that law, and we were growing further and further apart.

"What's wrong?" Romeo asked me one day. "You look like you don't wanna be doing this anymore."

I told him that I didn't. As usual Romeo didn't want to hear it.

"We ain't making those fools smoke no crack," he said. "If they ain't buying from us, they would buy from someone else."

I knew this was true, but when the crack boom happened. I really sat back and thought, do I want to be a part of this?

I was tired of the drug business. The plan had always been to keep moving. First candy, then cigarettes, then drugs, and now it was time for the next thing, for us to get into music videos, and real estate. But I'd been in this since nine years old, and it's hard to walk away from something you've been in your whole life. I loved the money, the street power. I loved that lifestyle. When you can walk into a very expensive store and order 10 pairs of $1,200 shoes. I would go downtown to Rubensteins and Brooks Brothers and spend $5,000. Or I might go to Miami or New York City and spend $30,000. Some guys meet a young lady and take her out to dinner, I would meet a young lady and buy her a car. I had my own selfish reasons to keep dealing drugs.

Plus, when you're in the position I was in, you can't just say, "I quit." Even if I were to say that, my enemies would still think I was a threat because I could always jump back in the game. So, what's their message? They get rid of me—they kill me. The only way out is if I leave the state. But I couldn't leave. Too many people depended on me to feed their families, too many people depended on me for making money. You have to remember, this was a business, and like any business, I had employees, and they depended on their jobs.

I also couldn't walk away from Montana. You're selling 50 or 60 kis of cocaine every few months for a Colombian drug lord, and you tell him, "I'm through with it." Nah-uh, that ain't happening. I would have needed to find a replacement for myself, but that's harder than it sounds. There are certain things you're not allowed to do. I couldn't just bring Lucky to the house, not if Montana hadn't invited him. You don't know how Lucky is going to turn out down the line. He might turn informant, or start doing crazy shit, bringing other people around, people whose phones might be tapped. Montana is going to remember that I brought this guy into his organization and put him at risk, and he'll blame me. With pressure like that, finding a replacement was impossible. I don't think Montana would have let me walk out anyway. I was doing too much business for him.

Around that same time, there were these young guys coming up, and watching them begin to walk the path I had walked was scary. There were these two guys in particular, Cowboy and Lil' Lawrence, and I was helping them out, they were both about 11-years-old. I made them go to school, like Goldy used to do for me. But you can't force someone to do something, you can only suggest it. I found out that when I left the school area, they left, too. Cowboy was square, but Lil' Lawrence was into the gangster life. I recall coming out of the projects one time and Lil' Lawrence was sitting there with Jo-Jo, smoking a blunt.

"What are you doing getting all messed up with him for, Jo-Jo?" I said. "He's too young."

"He brought the stuff to me," said Jo-Jo. "Lil' Lawrence likes smoking blunts."

I wondered how far this little one would go. I went to Romeo and got a gun and told him to take the bullets out. "Make sure they're out!" Then I said to Lil' Lawrence, "When Jo-Jo comes walking around that corner, I want you to shoot him in the head." I told Jo-Jo what was up so he wouldn't turn around and shoot Lil' Lawrence for real.

"You sure there's no bullets?" Jo-Jo said.

"Yeah," I said.

So Jo-Jo came around the corner, and there was Lil' Lawrence with the gun out. He aimed right at Jo-Jo's head and started firing: click, click, click.

CHAPTER EIGHT

ANYTHING GOES FOR NEW ORLEANS COPS

In the 1980s, you had a few cops selling drugs in New Orleans, but by the early '90s, they had begun putting together their own little police cartels. These guys were around our lifestyle all the time, and many of them were making $15,000 a year. We made that in a week, and cops wanted in on this money, so they got involved. One was a cop in the 5th District named Len Davis. Len set up his own drug dealing operation in the Projects, carried out by New Orleans Police officers and their henchmen.

Len had grown up in the Desire Projects. I remember hearing his mother had a food truck doing second lines and Mardi Gras. Guys robbed her truck, Len did nothing. He was a coward. As a kid, I never dealt with Len. I heard stories, though. My uncles used to whoop his ass, run him home from school. He was weak and didn't have a lot of friends in the Projects. He couldn't hack the street life, so he became a cop. But even as a cop Len had trouble gaining respect from people in the Projects. I think that's why he grew to hate us. We had the people's respect and the control he wanted. So Len learned to gain power and respect in other ways. He became ruthless.

I heard Len was fooling with this young lady, giving her money and jewelry he robbed from other gangsters. This young lady was also fooling with this guy named Spider. When Len found out Spider was dealing with her, he arrested him and charged him with selling drugs, even though he couldn't find any drugs. In the process, he broke Spider's jaw. That was how Len operated. He'd pull up, snap someone on the car, and arrest them. One time he grabbed a kid who must have been about 13. Len had him by the neck, and his mother came out there cursing, "Why'd you grab my son like that!?" Len told her to shut the fuck up.

"No," she said. "He's a good kid!"

Len started to arrest him, and people started coming out of their houses and taking pictures.

Respect is one of the few things you can't buy, and you can't force it on people either. You have to earn it. Len never understood that. The only thing he could do was instill fear, and the only reason he could do that was because he was a cop. Everyone knew, and he knew everyone knew that if he didn't have that badge on his uniform, he would be a dead son of a bitch. This guy had numerous complaints against him, and the New Orleans Police Department's Internal Affairs unit was covering it up. People asked Internal Affairs about Len, and they would say things like, "We're looking into it." But they never did anything. The problem with police Internal Affairs, it was still police. People in the Projects were watching though. They were especially watching how Len mistreated the young guys, and they were getting mad.

Len and his crew weren't just beating up little Project kids, they were into all kinds of shit. Say you were a legit businessman, running a nightclub, but your customers were all drug dealers, drug users, and pimps. What the cops would do is come in and tell everyone to throw their stuff on the ground. Then they'd walk around, pick up the drugs, and put it on whoever they wanted. Usually they'd put it on the owner. In order for them to not press charges, the owner would have to pay a certain amount of money. The cops did this regularly. About once a month, they shut down 3J's, the neighborhood club we'd been going to since we were kids. These guys would frame the owner with drugs, gather up the money, and go.

Nothing should surprise you. Anything went for New Orleans cops. They were falsifying documents, planting drugs on people, kidnapping, extorting. Drug dealers would hire cops to kill rival drug dealers. Or cops would kill someone uptown then bring the body downtown and leave it there. The first thing guys uptown would think is someone from downtown did the murder, and that maybe the guys from downtown were trying to start a war, perhaps so they could ease in and take over. But really the cops wanted to get all rival drug dealers out of the way, so *they* could ease in and take over.

Another tactic, cops knew we all had guns, so they'd roll up to the Projects, put everyone on the car, and pat them down. They wouldn't arrest us, just take our guns away. Then they'd leave and send someone into our neighborhood to start shooting, and we'd be defenseless. Or cops picked you up at a traffic stop, or somehow tricked you into getting in their car, and drove you around the city, then dropped you off in the middle of nowhere. Then they'd call one of their thugs to come out there and gun you down.

I've seen cases where guys had been shot and were lying on the ground bleeding to death, and the cops wouldn't help them. Cops would let guys die, especially if they had a record or reputation. A cop might be right there at the scene doing nothing, just waiting on the ambulance, knowing they were going to be about 30 or 45 minutes. They might even take their time calling the ambulance. Family members would be screaming at them and hollering. That's why if people have a car in this city, they take the victim to the hospital themselves. You can't rely on New Orleans police to help you out.

There is no such thing as an honest New Orleans cop. Even if a well-meaning person joins the police, as soon as they become a cop they become part of that corrupt system. Even if they aren't an actual participant in the corruption, they're still a part because their partners are a part, and they're going to turn a blind eye and not tell on their partners. Cops will stand up for one another, and they'll protect each other, even when other cops are doing illegal things. Especially when other cops are doing illegal things. And cops have the courts, at least in this city. What are you going to tell a prosecutor? What are you going to tell the state? You think they're going to take your word over the word of the cops? No way. No matter what they're doing, they are still cops, and you can't harm a cop, even if they are selling drugs and killing people.

By the early 1990s, murders were happening every day, and sometimes two and three a day. We were more at risk than ever before. People had all sorts of sneaky ways to get at you. Guys would lie under your car and wait for you to get in. Once you were sitting down, before you had the chance to turn the ignition on, they would jump up and shoot you through the window. Sometimes guys snuck into a car and hid in the backseat, when you opened the door—bam. I walked around the car once or twice before getting in. Checked to make sure no one was around the outside, no one was under the car, no one was inside. I stuck my key through the window and into the ignition to start the car, then got in.

Another big thing back then was guys dressing up as women. You wore a tight-fitting dress, low heels, and put on a wig. You didn't have to worry about makeup because women on the streets weren't wearing makeup back then, especially women of color, unless they were high up in an office somewhere. You might take what women called a spaghetti strap purse, not a big purse, but a small purse, and put your gun in there. Other guys would get a fake baby and put it in a carriage. If you're dressing like a mother pushing a stroller, you don't want to dress too sexy, because you want to look like a mother. You might wear a sundress and have a big diaper bag with all your stuff, and your gun might be in there or in the stroller. These women would walk up on you without you suspecting anything, then they'd take a gun, or several guns, out from under the baby carriage, or out of their purse, or out of the diaper bag, and shoot you.

In New Orleans, most houses are up on blocks, and some guys would lie under there all day long, waiting for someone to come home so they could kill them. That's one of the reasons I had different houses, and I never let anyone know where I stayed at. In the Projects, we started putting snipers on the roof for protection. The first Gulf War had just ended, and military guys were coming back who couldn't get jobs. So we gave them jobs. I had a Navy Seal train me in hand-to-hand combat and guerilla warfare. He wanted to teach me about rigging up explosives, how to blow up cars by running a wire from the engine to the gas tank. I told him I wasn't into learning that. But that was our world. I would put my bulletproof vest on over my pajamas just to put out the trash. I can't even explain how dangerous it was.

As Len Davis's drug dealing operation grew, suddenly we were in his way. We learned from Romeo that Len wanted to have a sit down with us. I said no, but Lucky wanted to see what he was all about. So we told Lucky, "Okay, you go." He came back and told us the news, Len wanted to start selling his shit in our Project.

"Fuck no," Romeo said. "If he wants a war, we'll give him a war."

For me getting out was starting to sound more and more like a good idea. I wanted to start legitimate businesses, and I wanted to get out of the city. I had always wanted to get some land, like 20 acres, and build a big old house with a 50-foot driveway off in the country, Lafayette or Opelousas. I could live my life and run my companies from there. I'd have a music business, and we could even start our own label and get into real estate. Buy all these old houses, fix them up and sell them or rent them out. I was still inspired by the vision of myself I had doing errands as a boy on Canal Street, of wearing nice slacks and shoes and controlling a powerful legitimate organization.

Lucky was on board, although he didn't want to move to the country. Romeo wasn't having any of it.

"Fuck no," he said. "I'm not running from the cops!"

"We are not running from the cops," I said. "We are getting out before it's too late." Little did I know, it was already too late.

The FBI had started following Len Davis and his crooked gang of cops in the 5th District. Through them, they overheard a conversation about us, and they thought, "Who are these guys?" I never talked about anything illegal on the phone or in the house or car. Cars can be bugged, and phones and houses, too. If the police came, I'd break my pager so they couldn't read the messages. You ask me about something illegal, I'm going to walk off. I won't accept money on the streets. If some guy goes to the store for me and brings change back, I won't accept the change. I played it very safe. But now thanks to these idiot cops, we were on the Feds radar.

The Feds had set Len up. They had him guarding a warehouse full of cocaine near the riverfront for a drug kingpin who was really an FBI agent. Len and more than a dozen other New Orleans police officers took shifts guarding the warehouse. Not only that, Len and his crew used police cars to drive the drugs around the city. Undercover agents rode with them, posing as dealers. It was hot during the day, and the cops guarding the warehouse had no air conditioning in their vehicles. They complained to the kingpin, and he gave them an air-conditioned van. But the van was wired to FBI headquarters. The Feds already had their phones tapped, and now they could hear every little conversation these crooked cops were having out there. At one point, Len even suggested killing the drug kingpin and taking all the coke.

This whole time, Len and his crew were still extorting and murdering people. And the Feds were listening in on it all. The Feds figured these guys were just a bunch of street level drug dealers, and they were letting them go about their business to build their case.

One day while I was in Miami, the cops' business got personal. My brother was murdered right outside my parents' front door. My mother was upstairs and heard the shots, and her and my father came running down. My brother had been shot 11 times. My mother bent down on the concrete and held him in her arms as he died. His death deeply affected her. She shut down completely. It still affects her. I don't think a parent ever gets over losing a son or daughter.

I came home right away, and Romeo picked me up at the airport. He told me some people had seen the boy who shot him run and jump in the back of a police car and that they saw Len Davis driving the car.

"You have no choice but to go to war now," Romeo said.

"Did you find out who the boy who shot him was?" I asked.

"Yeah, but we can't do anything to him," he said.

"Why?" I asked.

"Because he is dead, they killed him right after he did it."

"They who?" I asked.

"The fucking police, that's who," Romeo said. "Cop or not, Len has to go. He's not going to stop until we're all dead or in jail."

I went home to Tyra that night. She was hysterical. "They're going to get you next!" she said. "Let's move out of town. I lost all my brothers, and I'm not going to lose you!"

I didn't go to my brother's funeral because it was too much for me to handle. Turns out they had undercover cops there taking pictures. Before we could decide what to do about Len, him and his crew struck again. A woman living in the Lower 9th named Kim Groves had filed a complaint with Internal Affairs against Len and his partner for beating her nephew half to death. Even though the complaint was supposed to be secret, somehow Len found out, and he hunted her down.

The FBI got it all on tape. Len swearing and cursing about this woman, then planning one of the street guys he dealt with, Paul Hardy, his hitman, to do the murder, and afterward, when he got the call that the job had been done, celebrating. "Yeah, yeah, yeah!" said Len, "Rock-a-bye!" Kim, who was a mother of three, had been standing in front of her house, and Hardy shot her in the head with a single bullet. He executed her. The Feds could have put a stop to it then and there, or they could have stopped it before and saved this woman's life. But they didn't want to disrupt the investigation and jeopardize their case. The Feds wanted to make sure the evidence was strong enough to stick. Now they had more than they could have ever imagined, a uniformed New Orleans police officer ordering the execution of an innocent woman and then cheering her death. I don't think the Feds ever anticipated how crooked these cops really were.

In December 1994, the FBI arrested Len Davis and eight other police officers. The local papers were filled with it—and you can still look all this up with the FBI, because Len Davis remains in federal prison to this day. The whole city saw what we had seen and known all along. People who had never been involved with the law or hadn't come up in certain neighborhoods were shocked. But is this really shocking to you? You live in New Orleans, just open your eyes! A lot of the city had no idea that cops were dealing drugs and murdering people. This was something they never could have imagined.

Later the newspaper ran a front-page picture of Len and one of his partners in their underwear. The photo had been taken in a hotel room, where the cops had gone to meet an undercover FBI agent. This guy had stripped them down to make sure they weren't wired. The Feds had really outsmarted the police here. They were already listening in on the cops, but figured let's go the extra mile and make the cops worry about us thinking they are the ones who are bugged. So the Feds had these guys take their clothes off to show they weren't bugged. These cops were so brainwashed they did it, and now their naked-asses were on the front page of the paper.

This shows you how far these cops were willing to go to get what they wanted. They wanted the drugs they were guarding in that warehouse so bad that they didn't have any trouble agreeing to something as ridiculous as stripping off their clothes. So you see how it would be nothing for them to plant drugs on people, or execute rival drug dealers, or kill civilians in cold blood on the street. These cops were showing you what they were capable of right there.

The mayor, Marc Morial, made a big show of cleaning up the city. He hired a new police chief, Richard Pennington, who came up from DC just to straighten things out. Believe it or not, less than eight hours after Pennington was sworn into office, Kim Groves was murdered. Pennington took a look around and realized it was much worse than he thought. He had to do something quick, and the first place he went was the 9th Ward.

The Feds put informers in our Projects, and the FBI began following me. I was living in the East at that point, in a condo out on Roger Drive. One morning Tyra and I were at home having sex. She looked up, and there was a person looking right at her.

"Somebody's looking through the window!" she screamed.

I put my clothes on, grabbed my gun, and ran outside. These guys were up on my roof acting like they were fixing things.

"You have one minute to get down, or I'm going to start shooting!" I said.

The next day they had a guy back up on the light pole. At the time, I still didn't know I was dealing with the FBI. And now they were inside my bedroom.

CHAPTER NINE

SUPER BOWL, 1995

In the end, it wasn't the Feds who got to me. It was the crooked New Orleans police.

January 29, 1995 was the Super Bowl. The San Francisco 49ers played the San Diego Chargers, and Shelita and I were in the shower together getting ready for a party when the phone rang. I got out and picked it up. Nobody was there.

"Hello," I said. "Hello, hello…"

I was about to hang up when a voice said, "If you go to court on Len, we're going to kill you and your boys."

"Who the fuck is this!?" I said.

"Don't worry about who this is."

Even though the Feds had a strong case against Len, they always wanted more, and the crooked cops were worried about me testifying against Len in court. Although anyone who knew me knew I would never do that.

"Fuck you and fuck Len," I said. "I'm not a rat. And I hope Len does beat the charges, that way he can't get behind his badge and will have to face me on the streets, man to man." I hung up the phone.

The party was at the Hilton, and on our way, we dropped the twins, Daniella and Dana, who were about four months old at that time, off at my mother's house.

"Baby, what's wrong?" Shelita asked after I got back in the car.

"Nothing," I said.

"Don't tell me nothing," she said, "I can tell something's wrong with you."

"Are you a mind reader?" I asked.

"No, I'm not."

"Then how do you know I have something on my mind?"

"Because you haven't said one thing about this dress I have on!"

The dress was black and tight with a slit all the way up her leg. Shelita looked very sexy, but my head was somewhere else.

The party was in a suite, and everyone was there, Lucky, Romeo, and several other guys in our circle. Then you had guys from all over the city, driving up in Mercedes and Cadillacs, wearing crushed out Rolex watches. These weren't the type of guys who hung on the corner with their pants falling off. These were professional drug dealers, there to flex their financial muscles. Lawyers were there, too, and bail bondsmen, ex-ball players, local guys from the Saints, and beautiful women from all over the city. Some of the major political figures in the city were also there, and their wives and girlfriends.

Jo-Jo had spent a lot of money on the party. It was classy. There was shrimp, lobster, pork chops, red beans and rice, baked chilies, gumbo, beer, wine, champagne. There was also five strippers dressed up like San Francisco cheerleaders, giving lap dances and hand jobs. Jo-Jo is taking this shit too far, I thought to myself. I can recall that at one point the manager came up and said the music was too loud, five minutes later he was in there partying with us. And of course Romeo was doing his thing, eating women in the bathroom. I found out later that the informer was also at the party.

At one point, I pulled Lucky and Romeo aside and told them about the phone call, neither seemed to care.

"We're about to get out of this business," Lucky said.

"Fuck them," Romeo said.

The suite was on the top floor of the hotel, and while everyone else was enjoying themselves, I stood alone with a glass of champagne, looking out the window and down at the city. So beautiful, yet so violent. I was thinking about everything that was happening on each one of those side streets. I was thinking about my own life. I was flashing back. Even if I could get out of the business and change my life, there was still that one unsolvable problem. Which woman to pick, Tyra or Shelita?

Shelita was trying to get my attention that night but for all the wrong reasons. She wanted people to know she was there with me, and I was there with her. It was a status thing. She walked up behind me and whispered in my ear, "If you smile, I'll give you a kiss."

"You have to give me more than a kiss to make me smile," I said.

"I'll give you a lap dance," she said.

"Maybe later," I said.

"Do you want me to get you something to eat before it's all gone?" she asked.

"Yes," I said, without looking at her.

She brought me some stuffed eggs. Shelita knew I loved that. But when she set them down and I didn't eat any, she knew something was very wrong.

"I'm tired," she said. "Are you ready to go?"

On our way home, my pager went off, it was my mother. I called her up. "One of the twins won't stop crying," she said.

"Which one?"

"Dana."

"Okay," I said. "We're coming to get them."

"Just come and get Daniella," she said. "I'll keep Dana because y'all don't know how to treat a baby with colic."

So we stopped by my mother's house and picked up Daniella. Before we could get out of the neighborhood, my pager went off again. It was Yam, an old gangster who was selling drugs for me on the outskirts of the Projects.

"Man, come get this money before I go to bed," said Yam. Because of the Super Bowl, it had been a good day, and he had like $2,500.

"We have to stop by Yam's before going home," I told Shelita. She didn't like that.

"I'm tired," she said, "and we have this baby, and I don't like that neighborhood."

I kissed her a few times.

"Okay," she said, "but 10 minutes, that's it!"

In front of Yam's house, my pager went off again. It was Tyra. I tried to hide the number, but Shelita saw and started fussing. I ignored her, got out of the car, and began walking toward Yam's door. He had a padlock on his gate, and that made me pause. Yam being an older guy, he shut up shop early, and he put the lock on that gate to let people know he was done for the day. I had to page Yam to come out and open the gate. Maybe if I had been able to walk straight in, everything would have been different, or if I had gotten stopped at a red light on the way there, or left the hotel ten minutes later, or stayed at my mom's house ten minutes longer. But none of that happened. Instead I was standing by the gate waiting on Yam, and Shelita was looking at me all mad, and my daughter was in her lap, when we heard the shots: pow, pow, and then a third shot, pow.

Two guys came running around the corner with hoods tied over their heads and guns in their hands. The hoods were pulled so low you could only see their eyes. Even Shelita was scared. When she saw these guys, she started screaming. She figured they were coming to kill me. I was ready to defend myself. But these guys looked right at me and kept running. They had come from the direction of this little neighborhood spot called Creola's Bar.

"What happened?" Yam asked when he finally came out.

"I dunno," I told him. "Some fools around here."

He gave me my money. When I got back in the car, Shelita was still crying.

"They could have been coming for you!" she kept saying.

I wasn't concerned. Two guys shooting someone then running around the corner with their guns—I hate to say it, but that happens every day in this city. Shelita had hustled drugs on the streets, and she knew that better than anyone. But by me being so close to it, and her thinking that they might have been coming for me, and her having the baby in her lap, she was real shook up.

"I told you I don't like this neighborhood," she said, still crying. "Now you see why."

When we got home, I put on my big TV and thought about what had happened. *This is it, I have had enough of this shit. I'm out.*

Shelita went upstairs and put the baby to bed then came downstairs and sat next to me.

"I thought they were coming to kill you, baby," she said.

"Stop crying," I told her. "I'm alright. Go back upstairs and get in bed, I'll be up in a minute."

When she was gone, I kept thinking about the situation. Shelita was right to be worried. It was time for me to move on. But I knew that if I was going to give the streets up, I had to give Shelita up because Shelita was part of the streets. My path was becoming clear. I was getting out, which meant I was turning my back on Shelita. I called Tyra and told her what had happened.

"We need to get out of this city for a few days," she said.

"Where do you want to go?" I asked her.

"I don't know," she said.

"I need to have some fun," I said. "What about Disney World?"

"Okay," she said. "I'll make the reservation and see you in the morning." I hung up the phone.

The next day I was at Tyra's playing with my son. She jumped on my back, she was happy.

"We have a son, and you don't have a ring on your finger," I said. "Get down and let me talk to you."

She sat down and looked at me. I told her my plans to get out of the drug business and marry her. Tears ran down her face.

"What about Shelita?" she asked.

"It's just me and you," I said.

"You promise?"

"Yes."

"What about church, are you going to start coming with me to church?"

"Yes, I will go with you."

Just before leaving for Disney World, Tyra and I were lying in bed when her phone rang.

"It's for you," she said. It was Lucky.

"They got Romeo uptown last night," he said.

"Got him how?" I asked.

"He was leaving some ho's house and getting in his car. Two guys dressed up like women hit him about 30 times."

"What about the girl?" I asked.

"She set him up," Lucky said.

I hung up the phone and sat on the bed. Tyra looked at me, and I looked at the floor. She asked me what was wrong about five times before I told her. Romeo was a brother, more than a friend. We had started out in elementary school, we shared cereal together, we shared beds together. We had lived most of our lives together. We might not have always agreed with each other, but we were there for each other.

I had always known this was going to happen, but I didn't think it was going to happen that soon. Romeo was stubborn because his father was stubborn, his father was mean. I don't know what it is about that era of men, but it's the same thing with my father. They were mean, evil men. Maybe it was because of the system, them being held back by white society and not being able to do anything about it. You have to realize, the schools weren't de-segregated in this city until the 1960s, and on the first day, white women stood in line to throw rocks at the black students. Some bars in New Orleans weren't de-segregated until the 1980s. And there are still social clubs in this city, and minds in this city, that have never been desegregated. All that weighs on a man. And those men, my father and Romeo's father, that generation, they couldn't do nothing about it. So they came home and were mean with their families and with their kids. They took it out on us. And that hate and that meanness was then in us, too.

A few days later they buried Romeo. He had been shot so many times that they couldn't even open the casket. I wasn't there. I just couldn't handle it. Shelita went to represent me, and I stayed home with Tyra and my son. Strangely, just a few days after the funeral, someone robbed Romeo's father. I don't know if that was some weird sort of justice or what. But this man was stubborn to his dying day. He refused to give up his wallet, and they shot him, right in front of Romeo's mother. She had to run into the door of some store to keep from getting hit.

Tyra and I went to Disney World, and I totally forgot who I was and what I was into. I had never really had a childhood, and on that trip, for some reason, more so than any other time in my life, I became a kid. Normally I am not into rollercoasters, but when I got on them, then I really relaxed, I released all the anger, all the raw energy. And I kept riding. They had this rollercoaster called the Zipper. I think I rode that thing like five times. I would get off and get right back on. I went on Batman, I went on Splash Mountain. You get soaking wet on that ride, and I had money in my pocket, like two grand, but I didn't even care if it got wet. I forgot about the streets, I forgot about everything. I rode those rides practically until the place closed. I was running around having fun, and Tyra was looking at me like, "Are you serious, man?" But she was happy to see me happy.

I think we stayed at the Hilton. We had a big old suite, something like $300 a night for that room. One afternoon my pager went off, it was my mother's number with 911 at the end. That meant urgent, emergency call. We were still at the park, and I called from a pay phone to see what had happened.

"You're on America's Most Wanted," she told me, "for the murder of Murray Barnes." He's the person who had been shot outside of Creola's Bar the night of the Super Bowl.

I hung up the phone. That was the end of our vacation.

"You didn't do anything!" Tyra kept saying. "Go home, turn yourself in, and get a lawyer before they kill you!"

The next day we flew home, and I took care of all my business. I told Lucky to look after Shelita. Then I went back to Tyra. I figured I was looking at 60 to 90 days, that's what we were used to. I wasn't that worried. I was more pissed off. Why were these people doing this to me? I had no idea railroad tracks were being laid. Even though I thought I'd be seeing Tyra again in a few months, a couple months for a woman is a long time, especially if she has just given birth to your son. And Tyra didn't know the system like I did, so she assumed the worst. They had put me on America's Most Wanted after all.

The next day we made love for my last time as a free man, then Tyra and I went to the office of my lawyer, James Banks, on Carrolton Street, to turn myself in. Banks was our street lawyer. He handled our everyday problems with the police, legal documents, contracts. I'm driving and get a ticket, that's Banks's department. And a lot of times Banks would be in the car with me. If I got pulled over and the cop was verbally harassing me, I'd say, "Let me introduce you to my attorney."

Most of the time me and Banks were riding around, he'd be snorting coke. Go into his office, and he'd be there with three or four woman and drugs on the table. Banks was from the hood, he came from the Calliope Projects, and we got connected early on. This guy had a bar number, meaning he had passed the state bar exam and was a licensed lawyer in Louisiana. If you have a bar number, the sky is the limit in this city. Not too many police are going to fuck with you. We'd keep Banks loaded with drugs and women, and he'd be there for us when we needed him.

But I was beginning to think this case might be over his head. I was wanted for first-degree murder. The maximum penalty was death. We talked for a while, though, and Banks convinced me everything would be alright. What we were banking on was the simple fact that I didn't do it and that they had the wrong man. How could they find me guilty if I was actually innocent? We came up with a plan for me to turn myself in.

I knew a lot of the judges and bail bondsmen and lawyers in that courthouse, and I didn't want them to see me getting hauled into the police station. Not only that, I didn't want to be on the news in handcuffs for some shit I didn't do. Banks's strategy was to wait until the middle of the night. Just after one in the morning, he called the Homicide Division and said I was prepared to turn myself in. The cops told us to come to them, but we told them to come to us, and they did. They arrived around forty minutes later and read me my rights. I figured I'd turn myself in, and once they got the evidence straightened out, I would be on my way.

CHAPTER TEN

HARRY CONNICK AND ORLEANS PARISH

I was booked on first-degree murder and placed in Orleans Parish Prison, where I had first visited Goldy more than ten years before. Now he was at Angola, and I was the one in OPP. It was an old jail meant to hold hundreds of people, but there were thousands in there. They put me in a tier on the fourth floor for capital offenses—murder, kidnapping, rape, robbery. A tier is a big open room with a line of beds stacked three on top of one another against the wall.

The state has 60 days to present their case before a grand jury, and during this time, you are kept in OPP. Then a grand jury examines the evidence and decides whether to let you go or bring an indictment and proceed with the case. I figured when my 60 days was up they'd cut me loose. But on about my 60th day, the police woke me up and said to get ready for court.

These assholes were actually going to put me in front of a grand jury. I couldn't believe it.

I knew two guys on my tier, Manny, who was from the Florida Projects, and Wine, from the Calliope Projects. I woke Manny and told him to call Tyra and tell her to meet me in court. OPP is connected to Orleans Parish Criminal District Court. I put on my prison issued uniform, orange pants and an orange shirt, and they put me in handcuffs and shackles and brought me into Courtroom F. I hadn't heard from Banks since getting to OPP, and when I got into court, he wasn't there. Where the fuck was he? Probably getting loaded or high with some women.

The Judge was Dennis Waldron. He used to be an assistant District Attorney, which is how it works in Orleans Parish. Serve time as a DA in the office of Harry Connick, who was the head DA back then, and if you win your cases and push hard, you'll probably become a judge. But you still have the connection to the DA's office, and you're still loyal to Connick.

To give you an idea of what kind of shop Connick was running as head DA: in 1994, two years before my trial, a case involving Connick's office went all the way to the Supreme Court. Justice David Souter tore these New Orleans prosecutors apart, saying Connick's office had "descend[ed] to a gladiatorial level unmitigated by any prosecutorial obligation for the sake of the truth." And in 2011, another case from my time, this guy named Juan Smith goes to the Supreme Court. This time the justices conclude in an 8 to 1 decision that evidence that could have helped Smith was suppressed by prosecutors in Connick's office, and that they also presented false or misleading evidence to help convict him. Strike two for Connick.

In another case from my era, this man named John Thompson was convicted of murder under Connick's office and served 14 years on death row. As was typical with Harry Connick's office, the prosecutors had evidence proving he was innocent but kept it hidden from the defense. They actually had a piece of bloody clothing from the crime scene that didn't match up to Thompson, it matched up to some other guy. But the prosecutor didn't reveal this valuable piece of evidence until he was on his deathbed. When he finally gets out, Thompson sued Connick and his gang for $14 million, a million for every year this innocent man sat rotting on death row. In 2012 the case about whether or not the city needs to pay Thompson goes to the Supreme Court. You'd think these justices would get wise to the fact that they keep seeing the same faces in their courtroom. But somehow the majority of these justices don't see it that way and don't come down agreeing Thompson should get the money. But in the minority opinion, Justice Ruth Bader Ginsburg tears Connick apart, "Connick, who himself had been indicted for suppression of evidence," Ginsburg writes, "created a tinderbox in Orleans Parish in which...violations were nigh inevitable." And she continues: "The evidence in this case presents overwhelming support for the conclusion that the Orleans Parish Office slighted its responsibility to the profession."

That's who I was dealing with. You think there's any way me, or any human being convicted in Orleans Parish for that matter, is going to get a fair trial with these ignorant "gladiators" running the show? Hell no. Connick was going to win and get a conviction by any means necessary, even if he had to lie and make up evidence. And if Connick made a call saying, "We need this guy off the streets," the judge listened.

Connick's mind was still locked in the 1950s, and although his name was respected in the city, it was respected in the circles that thought like him. In fact Connick himself even said that he had "stopped reading law books" when he was first elected District Attorney in 1974. Can you imagine that? This man hired by the public to uphold the law last read a law book at a time when there were still bars and society clubs in this city where black people were not welcome. I learned later that Harry Connick issued trophies, at the end of each year, to judges who tried the most cases. In Orleans Parish, convicting people was like a sporting competition.

To even call Orleans Parish judges, *judges*, is misleading. These guys were really just extensions of the DA's office. There were judges we knew were independent of Connick and the DA's office, like Marullo, who we were used to dealing with, or Keva Johnson. These were the liberated judges, they followed their own path, and Marullo in particular hated Connick. Guys prayed to go in front of Marullo or Johnson. Say you got busted with drugs. Marullo would send you to rehab before sending you to prison. From what I saw,

Connick had a three-strikes-and-you're-out attitude. Once you had your strikes, in his eyes, you couldn't be rehabilitated. All the judges tied to him seemed to think the same way.

I didn't know so much about this dude Waldron. He was a young-looking white guy with some sort of, I wouldn't call it a disease, but a mental disorder. He had to count everything. When he walked, he had to count his steps, and you could see him mumbling to himself as he walked. In court I noticed that he was mainly counting the clock on the wall. This guy loved counting clocks. He looked something like Dennis the Menace, and I saw right away he was going to be a real asshole.

I sat down, and a female prisoner I didn't know was told to stand and come to the bench in the case of The State vs. Dan Bright and Christina Davis in the murder of Murray Barnes.

"How do you plead?" the court asked her.

"Not guilty," she yelled out.

I looked at Tyra, who was seated behind me with the other courtroom visitors. "What the fuck is going on?" I called to her. "Who is that woman?"

"I don't know," she said.

"Go and find Banks," I told her. "And tell his ass to come see me today."

Tyra got up and left. As she was walking out of the courtroom, I was reminded of just how sexy she was. She wore a long brown tight-fitting dress with her back out.

"Mr. Bright, how do you plead, guilty or not guilty?" the judge asked.

This is a dumb question.

"Not guilty!" I yelled out.

"Can you afford a lawyer?" he asked.

"Yes, I can," I said.

I still couldn't believe I was getting indicted. As the police was walking me back to my tier, I asked him who the woman on the stand was. He looked at me, "That's your co-defendant."

"My co-defendant!?"

Now I was worried. How the fuck could I have a co-defendant when I didn't kill anyone? Initially I thought Banks would be fine, but after getting indicted, I knew he had to go. No way I was going to trial with Banks, coming in there all drunk and coked up. This case was over his head. Plus Banks was my street lawyer, he was connected to me, and I was concerned that if I went to trial with him, it might hurt me.

I should have kept Banks though because I ended up going to trial with a drunk anyway. On the phone that night, Tyra was going on and on about how her mom knew a good lawyer, and eventually I said, "Okay, let's try him." We met in the attorney-client meeting room on the second floor of OPP. This lawyer looked like a bum. He was short, with curly black hair, and wore an old wrinkled suit and rundown shoes. His name was Robert Oberfell. We talked for like ten minutes then he disappeared. I went straight to the phone and called Tyra.

"Man, what kind of lawyer you hook me up with?"

"He's a good lawyer!" she said. "He got my brother out."

What I didn't know is Oberfell had never actually gone to trial before his cases had either been dismissed for lack of evidence, or he had made plea-bargains. And I was his first death row case.

Shelita could get me more information than this idiot lawyer, and I called her later that night. "Find out who this Christina Davis is," I told her.

"Why?" she asked.

I explained what had happened.

"Baby, they trying to railroad you!"

"I can see that," I said. "Just find out who Christina is."

I was up all night trying to figure out what was going on and who was behind it. I knew something was wrong because in order to get indicted, you need a witness to go in front of the grand jury. So who was this witness who saw me do this thing I didn't do?

The next day was visiting day. Tyra came first. "The lawyer wasn't in his office, but I'll keep trying to call him," she said. "I know you are feeling down and lonely, but I have something that will cheer you up."

"What?" I asked. "A get out of jail free card?"

"No," she said. "God is going to get you out. I been praying every night."

I was mad. We only have 15 minutes to talk, and she comes wanting to talk about God. Here Shelita was out there on the streets gathering intel and doing everything she could to help me, and Tyra just wanted to put it in God's hands. But she had something else. Tyra was wearing a long, black tight-fitting dress with the back out and turned around to show me a tattoo with my name on her shoulder: *Poonie*.

I smiled. "When did you do that?"

"Last week," she said. "I thought you saw it when I was in court yesterday."

"No, I was looking at your ass," I said.

"You is so nasty," she said, smiling.

"Time's up," said the police.

"I love you," she said. "Call me when you think I made it home." She walked off. Thirty minutes later, Shelita came.

"What did you find out?" I asked.

You have to remember, New Orleans is a small city, and if you're in touch with the streets, you can find out anything. There was a cop Shelita was real cool with, and he was giving her information. Still, what she was saying wasn't making me feel any better about my situation.

"Christina Davis lives in that neighborhood," Shelita said, "and they said she was at the bar and told the man to go outside. They are saying she set him up so you could rob him."

"What the fuck do I need to rob him for, baby?"

"I know that, I was with you," she said. "And I talked to the police I know, he told me they know you didn't do it, but they want you off the streets, and this is the charge against you."

"Who the fuck is *they*?" I asked her.

"The DA, and the Chief of Police," she said. Like I've been saying, not only did I have Len and his corrupt circle of cops against me, Pennington and Morial were cleaning up the city and wanted me out of the way—and even if Morial didn't actively participate, he didn't do anything to stop them.

"They also told me they had a witness who was going to lie," Shelita said, "and say he saw you kill that man."

"Find that fucking lawyer," I told her, "and tell him what you told me."

"Time's up," the police said.

Shelita left, and I went back to the tier and sat on my bed. Manny came over and asked if I was alright.

"I'm being set up," I told him.

But being locked in OPP, there wasn't much I could do about it. As the weeks and months slowly dragged on, I waited for my trial date and waited for my lawyer to come and visit me. The fourth floor of OPP was nice because you could look out the windows onto the streets below and see the scene out there. Each side of the tier had windows, and the windows on my side looked out at this McDonald's they used to have on the corner of Broad and Tulane. I would tell Tyra when to come, and she'd take my son to the parking lot and stand there just so I could see them. From where Wine was, the tier looked down into the prison parking lot, where the police parked their cars. Some guy from Uptown had a bunch of girls coming in this parking lot, dancing and shaking, taking their clothes off. I'd ask the guards to go see Wine so I could look out that window. These women would be buck naked, twerking right there in the parish prison parking lot. The cops didn't care. They might run these women off, but they'd come right back.

Tuesday was visiting day, and everyone saw their families. Tyra would usually bring my son, who we called Lil' Man. He was getting big. He still couldn't walk, but he could stand, and it made me very happy to see him. Visiting day was also when drugs came in, mostly weed. OPP was such an old raggedy building that the place was filled with holes. In the visiting room, there wasn't glass separating the prisoners from the visitors. It was more like a small screen, like chicken wire. It was easy to punch a hole through the screen and stick something through, say a little pouch of weed. In the tier after visits was like one big party, with everyone smoking weed. We would cut the shower on so the steam would hide the smoke, and guys would blow Johnson's baby powder into the air to kill the scent. Tyra snuck me pictures through that screen, too. Not nude, pictures of her in biker shorts or board shorts, or an underwear and bra. One thing I was always thinking about: who was taking these damn pictures?

Mostly I was thinking about my case or talking with someone on the phone about my case. Each tier had payphones on the wall, and you could call collect. I didn't call Tyra that much. Shelita was more in tune. She'd tell me what was going on with the streets and at the court. Shelita was still out there making money so I didn't have to worry about her paying the bill. I was regularly sending Shelita over to see my lawyer, Oberfell. Either he wasn't in the office, or if he was, he'd say he was going to come see me soon and never come. Later I found out why he wasn't coming. The guy was an alcoholic, and he liked coke. I kept kicking myself for listening to Tyra.

For months I waited eagerly to go to court. Even though my lawyer was turning out to be a complete moron, I still had hope because I knew I hadn't done anything.

Shelita and I talked on the phone, but she would come on visiting day, too, although she was starting to look different. Her face had become fat, and her eyes were red. People didn't know what was going on with her. They were going around saying she had HIV. Then the doctors started treating her with steroids. She got fat. I mean she blew up. Those steroids made her look like a damn body builder. Every time I talked to her on the phone, she'd tell me she was tired. She didn't visit for like a month.

"Get your ass up here," I told her. "I want to see you."

Eventually she came. Shelita had to come up a bunch of steps to get to the visiting room, and when she got in, she was breathing real hard. I didn't even recognize her. She was big, and her face was swollen. She still had that toughness about her, but you could see she was changed, and she was tired just from climbing some stairs.

"Bitch, are you pregnant?" I asked.

She looked at me and started crying. "I have lupus."

"What is lupus?" I asked her, shocked, "and how did you get it?"

Lupus is a disease of the immune system. Your body attacks its own tissues and organs.

"They don't have a cure for it," Shelita said. "It's fatal."

"FUCK!" I said.

"Baby, I'm dying," she cried.

"Time's up," the police said.

"Man, let me talk to her for five more minutes."

"Can't do that," the police said.

"Baby, call me tonight," she said, and left.

I looked at her walking off and felt bad because I couldn't help her. I couldn't even hold her. For the next few days, all I thought about was Shelita. I couldn't be there for her, and she was doing so much for me, even though she was sick, even though she was dying.

Not long afterward, I got a call from the police telling me that I had a visitor. What now, I thought, someone else in my life is dead or dying? But when I got to the attorney-client meeting room, I saw two white guys sitting at a table with a lot of pictures and a tape recorder. It was the FBI.

"Have a seat, Mr. Bright," one of them said. "We want to show you something."

They showed me photos of everyone in my crew, then played a tape. It was Lucky and a guy talking about killing Jo-Jo. Then they played another tape, of Lucky and a cop. The cop was telling Lucky how much coke he had and what he was going to sell it for. He told Lucky he wanted to be his right-hand business partner.

"All that sounds good," Lucky said. "But can you keep the police off my back?"

"This is not a problem," the cop said, "as long as you stay in the 9th Ward."

All the while the tape was playing, the FBI agents were looking at me to see my reaction.

"Man, what the fuck does this have to do with me?" I asked.

"We know you did not kill Mr. Barnes," they said. "Now if you help us, we will help you."

"I don't know any of these people you are showing me," I said.

"Are you sure, Mr. Bright?"

And before I could say anything, the other agent pulled out more photos. Me and Lucky standing in the projects, me and Lucky at the Super Bowl party, me and Lucky leaving his house, me and Lucky playing with my son, me and Lucky having dinner, me and Lucky in New York, Miami, Baton Rouge. They had photos of everything.

"We know you are being set up," one of them said. "We also know you are not going to walk out of that courtroom a free man. So are you going to help us or not?"

It was more scare tactics. The Feds had a lot on Len and his crew, but they could always use more, and they wanted me to rat. These guys figured by showing me all these photos and playing these tapes, they could convince me that sooner or later someone in my crew would give me up. I was on edge, but I never let them see it. I knew Shelita wasn't going to rat on me. I knew Lucky wasn't going to rat. But that's all I could speak for. I rarely dealt with the rest of the crew. Lucky dealt with them, and I would deal with Lucky. If the Feds started waving offers in front of their face, I didn't know what they might do. The information I could have provided them would also help bring a lot of people down, streetwise, and politics-wise. Still it was not in my blood to do that.

"I will die before I become a rat," I told the FBI agents. "You guys have a nice day."

One morning, about a week after the FBI visited me, I was lying in bed when Manny ran over.

"Poonie, come look at the news!"

"What's on the news?" I asked him.

"It's your people," he said.

My whole crew was on TV. The Feds had busted everyone. Lucky was labeled as the boss. I looked on in disbelief then went and sat on my bed. "I'm next," I thought. But they never came. The FBI had rushed their investigation. If they had taken their time and kept us under surveillance, I think they would have had enough evidence to get everyone. But the Feds were bringing down two major organizations, the crooked cops and us. And after Len Davis killed Kim Groves, the Feds had to prematurely shut down their operation.

I figure the Feds told the state something like, *You've got nothing on him, he didn't do the crime you have him in on*. And the state probably ignored them, or told them to screw off, said that they didn't want to hear it. That was an election year, and the mayor and DA were up for reelection. The state didn't want to turn me over to the Feds. They probably wanted to use me as a political prize. And the Feds probably figured they would get me after the trial was over. They didn't think the murder charge would stick. They figured I'd be proven innocent of murder in state court then walk right into their handcuffs and be taken to federal court on drug charges. But the Feds didn't know the extent of the corruption they were dealing with down here. This wasn't just some typical corrupt-ass Southern politics. This was Harry Connick and Orleans Parish.

A long time later, I learned what really happened that night. Murray Barnes stopped by Creola's to see if he had won a Super Bowl betting pool. He and his friend Kevin Singleton went in to check while his cousin, Freddie Thompson, stayed in the truck. Kevin poked his head out and yelled to Freddie to come in. Murray had won the pool and was going to buy everyone drinks. As Freddie was getting out of the truck, Christina Davis came around, asking him where Murray was. The state later tried to make this all suspicious, but really Christina just wanted to talk to Murray because she was a thief. Thieves steal things in the sizes of their customers, and Christina occasionally stole things for Murray. She had two jogging suits for him.

The bartender gave Murray two envelopes, each containing $500. Kevin, Freddie, and Murray all had some drinks and then came back out to Murray's truck to go home. Murray was the last one in, and it was while he was about to get in the truck that two guys came out of the alley and approached him. He took off running toward the bar, and they shot him in the back and, without taking any of the money, ran off in the other direction. I was around the corner, standing by Yam's gate, waiting for him to open up. I heard the shots and then saw the two guys run by with hoods on their heads.

Later that night, the homicide detectives got to interviewing people. One of the cops at the scene was

Detective Michael Mims. Mims wasn't part of Len's drug operation, but they still hung together, and Mims had to know how corrupt Len was. That night Mims had interviewed a woman from the neighborhood named Thais McKay, and Thais had mentioned that she had seen me in the area. Thais was a drug addict, and she wasn't a reliable person. I don't think she was trying to frame me, she was just telling the officer who she had seen. Mims then told the head Homicide Detective, Arthur Kaufman, the names of people who were in the area. And one of those names was mine.

I don't know who it was, but someone in that chain of cops must have known me, and probably was connected to Len, too, and figured, "Hey, this is a real nice way for us to get Dan." Even though Len and a lot of his crew were locked up, you have to remember there were many other police officers involved in what he was doing, and it's possible they were still out to do him a favor. As far as who exactly was the one who said, "Let's pin this on Dan," I don't know.

I knew the local cops like Len, but I had never heard of this Detective Arthur Kaufman. Turns out he was one of the most corrupt guys on the force. He wasn't out on the streets murdering and dealing like some of these cops, he was more arranging things behind the scenes, coercing witnesses into saying what the state wanted them to, faking evidence, rigging the system. Detective Kaufman went to visit Thais McKay at OPP. She had been brought in on some charge or other, and he wanted to try and push her into saying that I had actually done the murder. She told him again and again,

Dan didn't do it, and Kaufman kept pressing her. We know what Thais told him thanks to a later interview with her by an Orleans Indigent Defender investigator. Kaufman also asked her about Christina Davis, and she told the investigator, and I quote, "Christine is a dirty low down bitch, but I don't think she had nothing to do with it. As far as setting somebody up or robbing somebody, she ain't got it in her." According to what Thais told the Indigent Defender investigator, Kaufman laughed. Suddenly she didn't seem like such a great eyewitness to these crooked cops, and that is why they never subpoenaed her.

But Kaufman found another way to stick the murder on me. He had Freddie Thompson come down to the police station to identify the suspect. Man, Freddie Thompson looks like the kind of guy you give quarters to in front of the bars downtown. I don't mean to sound harsh, but he had his own rap sheet. He had been arrested for burglary. But the state suppressed that and didn't let my lawyers or the jury know. The night of the murder, Freddie had been drinking for twelve hours straight. And by being drunk, he was breaking his parole. This clown is who the state decided to make their star witness.

Once Kaufman had Freddie at the station, all he had to do was show him a lineup with me in it. The police use a tactic where they'll get a lineup of six photos and tell someone, "Now, you look at this one real good," and they will tap the picture of the person they want to be charged so your eye is drawn to it. A lot of the times they might have a ring on the finger they are using to tap with so your eye is even more drawn. You're thinking, "Well they are the police, they know what they are doing, so I guess it was that guy." And you have to remember, thinking in general is like a foreign language to Freddie. One way or another, they got him to finger me as the suspect. The only problem was that Kevin Singleton was also shown a police lineup of six people by Detective Kaufman. I was one of those six. But Kevin couldn't identify the murderer.

Christina Davis's lawyer was a real sleek man with this Arabian playboy type look named Hans Sinha. Sinha was 6'1 or 6'3, slick black hair, professional, he just had this swag about him. Sinha was filing motion after motion, based on all the different errors he saw the detectives and state had made in the case. He was the one doing all the strategizing, and Waldron took him seriously. My lawyer was just going along with whatever Sinha said. He wasn't doing any work on the case. He didn't file one damn motion during the entire 16 months leading up to the trial. I had the wrong lawyer. He did nothing. He just got drunk. The worst part was Sinha was free. He was court appointed. And I was paying money for this fool. I am sure Sinha knew it was a setup, and that neither of us had anything to do with the crime. And at the beginning of August, based on motions Sinha had filed, we had a hearing.

A lot of things came out at this hearing. Oberfell was cross-examining Kaufman on the stand, and he said he only showed a photo lineup to one witness. Then Kevin Singleton, the state's own witness, came up and said that Kaufman also showed him a photo lineup, but he was unable to make an identification. Kaufman was brought back up and said he didn't remember showing Kevin Singleton lineup photos. Judge Waldron was busy counting his clocks, but even he was questioning the evidence and beginning to get suspicious. Waldron said that if Kevin Singleton was shown photos with me in the lineup but did not identify me, and I quote from the hearing transcript, "that would be Brady material. Clearly, it would be Brady."

By Brady he is referring to a 1963 Supreme Court decision, which said that if the prosecution has evidence that potentially shows the innocence of the defendant, they are obligated to turn that evidence over to the defense. Connick's office didn't like turning over that evidence, and he really didn't even understand what the Brady ruling meant, that's why so many of his cases later ended up getting reviewed by the Supreme Court. But at that point in the hearing, it was looking like Waldron was on my side regarding this matter. Just a little bit earlier in the hearing, Waldron had actually said, and again, I quote from the transcript:

I'm searching for—what is it—this is an unusual case, and I normally don't ask these questions. What is it that you allege forms the basis for either of these persons being charged with murder? So far I've heard nothing…I just don't see anything yet. And I'm not saying you don't have something. I just haven't heard it. What is it that you allege either of these persons did to cause the death of the gentleman?

I was surprised. The judge didn't seem to be corrupted. He was clued in, paying attention to the evidence the attorneys were presenting him with, and wondering why the hell I was up here being charged with this murder. But the prosecutor, Mary Glass, was starting to get real shaky. She requested an in camera inspection with Judge Waldron so she could show him this supplemental report, which contained the police write-up of the case. This means she went into the judge's chamber with Waldron but without my lawyer or Sinha. That's illegal, and grounds for a mistrial. And we had no idea what happened in there because it wasn't recorded. But suddenly the judge came back out and was like a new man. He said, and again I quote:

> Following an in camera inspection, the Court is satisfied that there was probable cause for the arrest based on the totality of the information provided to the Magistrate, that there appears to be no discrepancy in what was said under oath to the Magistrate by Detective Kaufman in connection with the arrest warrant for each person.

I was like, what the hell just happened?! This guy got a split personality or something, like Jekyll and Hyde? From that moment on, he was a different judge. What probably happened in his chambers was that the prosecutor showed Waldron the police write-up, which stated that the police connected my name to the crime from an anonymous phone call placed to the Homicide Office. Come on, man! The anonymous call was complete bullshit. It was just to give them proper cause to arrest me, and it was probably made by a police officer who just wanted to collect the Crimestoppers reward. In fact one of my lawyers later on hypothesized that the anonymous caller may have even been Kaufman himself. The anonymous call was also overkill, although these dumbass prosecutors didn't realize it. Why do you need an anonymous call if you already have an eyewitness testifying that I did the murder? Why not just take him down to homicide and see if he can ID me?

If you have any type of common sense, you can sit down and read the transcript for this case and see it just doesn't read right. In legal terms, the anonymous call is called hearsay because there is no real proof anyone ever actually gave this information. And you can't build a case on hearsay. But this is exactly what the police and prosecutors did. In fact creating proper cause in cases when they have none is an old NOPD trick.

The exits were being sealed, the railroad track was being laid. And when the day came, there was no way I was going to walk out of that courtroom a free man. Still, for some reason, I was convinced I had a chance.

CHAPTER ELEVEN

THE TRIAL, BEFORE LUNCH

On Monday July 1, 1996, the trial was to begin. I had been in OPP for almost a year and a half and hadn't spoken to my lawyer for more than 20 minutes. On the Friday before the trial, he finally visited.

"Everything is looking good," he told me.

"Hold up," I said. "We haven't even prepared a defense or discussed who the witnesses are going to be."

"I'm taking care of all that," he said.

"Man, this is my life on the line!" I said. "I haven't seen your ass in a year, and now you come here two days before the trial without a proper defense. We're supposed to be discussing strategy."

We talked for about 20 minutes, then he left.

"I'll come back and see you before the trial," he said.

"How you going to come see me if the trial is Monday?"

"I'll come back tomorrow," he said. Of course he never showed.

Back on the tier, Manny and Wine asked me what was up.

"Trial is Monday, that's what's up," I said.

I called Shelita and asked her if Oberfell had talked to her or Yam.

"No," she said.

"How the fuck is he going to prepare a defense without you or Yam?"

"I don't know, but we will be there," she said. "Baby, I don't like this lawyer, it looks like he's going to sell you out. Where'd you get him?"

"From Tyra's mother," I said.

"You know that woman doesn't like you!" she said. "Why didn't you use your own lawyers?"

"Because I wanted a lawyer the DAs couldn't link to me," I said. But she was right. For all I knew, Tyra's mother had set me up with a bad lawyer on purpose.

Monday rolled around, and then began what was surely one of the fastest trials in Louisiana history. The first day was jury selection. Typically you have several dozen jurors in the courtroom, and it's the job of the defense attorneys and prosecutors to ask questions of individual jurors and, based on their answers, decide who they want on the jury. This is a critical part of any trial, and there's a lot of strategizing involved. Usually it takes three or four days to pick a jury, and for a death penalty case, it might take two or three weeks. My jury was picked before lunchtime on the first day of jury selection.

During the selection process, my attorney was pretty much asleep. The DA eliminated all jurors opposed to the death penalty and rigged the jury with people tough on crime and willing to believe whatever the government told them. If you could have seen this jury, man, a three-year-old could have influenced them. One juror was about six-months pregnant, sitting in the jury box with her big belly. She didn't want to be there. There was a black guy who slept through the whole trial and woke up twice to give his verdicts. And there was a guy who looked like a cop. We found out later he *was* a former undercover cop and a current employee of the New Orleans Police Department. This guy was put there to make sure the prosecution got a conviction, and he was real forceful in sharing his opinion with other jurors. The only one who took the trial seriously was the jury foreman, a short, casually dressed woman named Kathleen Hawk Norman.

"We are aware of the holiday weekend that's coming," Judge Waldron told the jury. "We have been assured by the attorneys that the case would be finished by Wednesday with ample time for everyone to be gone that evening, if anybody has plans for going out of town or anything."

I couldn't believe my ears. What kind of judge assures the jury that a murder trial will only last two days? Up until that moment, I was still naive enough to think I was going to receive a fair trial. The jury would hear the evidence and do the right thing. But he was speaking as if the outcome of the case had already been decided.

Waldron spent a lot of time talking to the jury about the difference between first-degree murder, second-degree murder, and manslaughter. I think he more or less wanted to flex his intellect here. But me being ignorant of the law at that time, I didn't understand what was happening. I didn't realize that he was basically outlining the recipe for a sure conviction. Even my idiotic lawyer was talking over my head. And no one had bothered to tell me that Christina Davis and I were going to be tried separately. It was my trial, and it was like I didn't even exist.

There was a new lead DA, Karen Herman, and she was a pit bull. Herman wasn't going to let anything stop her from getting a conviction. I don't know if she knew I was actually innocent, or if she was just taking orders, but when you have a pit bull, it doesn't matter. You already know her bloodline, cut her loose and she's going to fight. And she's going to win by any means necessary, even if it means breaking the law she swore to uphold. And those above her knew how hungry she was. Before we broke on the first day, Herman read her opening argument, which laid out the case against me. Her story was not that convincing, but the way this jury was rigged up, she didn't need much evidence.

"I would submit to you, ladies and gentleman," Herman said, "that the motive for this crime was to take that money from Murray Barnes...I would submit to you that this crime was committed during the attempted perpetration of an armed robbery, and when it was committed, Dan Bright had the specific intent to do it. He had the specific intent to kill or inflict great bodily harm by shooting Murray Barnes in the back three times. He's guilty of first-degree murder, and I'm going to ask you to come back with that verdict, probably tomorrow afternoon—thank you."

She sounded so arrogant, but really all the state had on me was a bullshit anonymous call and a drunk eyewitness. As for Oberfell's opening argument, he waived it. This is a first-degree murder case, what kind of defense attorney waives his opening argument? That's supposed to lay the format down for the whole trial.

On the second day, the trial began real early, about 8:30am. I was wearing dark dress trousers and a short sleeve sport shirt along with some fancy dress shoes. The court allows you to wear whatever clothes you want, so as not to influence the jury, and my mom had brought me the outfit the day before. Oberfell was wearing his usual rundown penny loafers, a dark gray suit, wrinkled and too big, his papers spilling out everywhere. When I walked in the courtroom, he was talking to Karen Herman. He saw me and stopped talking.

"What were you all talking about?" I asked him.

"Nothing about the case," he said. He was drunk. I could smell the alcohol on him.

"Why did you waive your opening argument?"

"I know what I'm doing," he said.

I looked at him. "You better."

I glanced around the courtroom. My mom was there, my sister was there. Tyra and Shelita were there, both dressed real professionally. My father didn't come, but that wasn't a shock. My grandmother didn't come, she was too sick. Cousins and aunts on my mother's side were there. Women from around the city—most of them I had had sex with—peeped their heads in and waved. Rumors had circulated that I was being rail-roaded, and bail bondsmen and lawyers I knew were dropping in to shake my hand, "Good luck, I heard they got you bad." Others were more critical, "Why'd you call him!" they asked, pointing at my pathetic lawyer. "Why didn't you call us?" And again I kicked myself. Why had I listened to Tyra and her mother?

The judge watched all these Project people come in, with their expensive watches and shoes. I remember someone came in with a Rolex with crushed out diamonds everywhere and big earrings with diamond studs. People had to stay outside in the hallway because the courtroom was too packed. The judge didn't like any of it one bit. "Clear my hallway!" he yelled, and banged on his gavel. He had never seen that many people coming for one defendant. Court officials looked at me like, "Who is this guy?" But Herman knew who I was and made sure to tell the judge, "Black organized crime, your honor, this is what you're witnessing, the Black mafia."

Meanwhile Tyra and Shelita were already going at it, arguing over which one should be there and which one shouldn't.

"I'm his wife!" Tyra screamed. "She's just a ho."

Shelita just smiled and laughed and gave Tyra the finger.

"Oh lord," my mother said.

I'm going to kill both of these knuckleheads, I thought to myself.

There was a woman there I had been sexing for about two months. I think we met at the mall or something. Suddenly she entered the courtroom, and she gave her gun and badge to the officer at the door. I could have shit myself. This bitch is police! She came over and gave my lawyer a letter for me. As she was walking back to her seat, we made eye contact, and she smiled. "Good luck," she whispered. Good luck my ass, I thought. Before the trial began, I opened the letter and started reading:

Dan,
I have been a police officer for two years. I always heard your name from other officers and wanted to meet you for myself. They all made you out to be so bad. The day I met you was not an accident. I followed you, so when you saw me in the mall I smiled and rolled my eyes hoping you would come and flirt with me and you did. One thing led to another and I forgot I was a police officer, Dan. I really wish you good luck. When you read this letter please rip it up.

I looked across the courtroom at her and ripped up the letter. She smiled and said, "Thank you."

"All rise," a court officer said, and the jury came in. The first witness was Genora Bickham, the bartender at Creola's. She knew I didn't hang in that bar. I didn't go in hole-in-the-wall neighborhood bars where I could get jammed up. She knew I wasn't there that night, so she wasn't much use to the state, and was only on the stand a few minutes.

Next was the coroner, Dr. Paul McGarry. Herman made him go through the gruesome details of Murray Barnes's bullet wounds. This was to build sympathy with the jury and make the killer out to be a real cowardly individual, since Barnes was shot three times in the back. At one point while Herman was questioning McGarry, my lawyer took his briefcase and walked out of the courtroom, and the trial just continued on without him. Everyone was looking for him, and eventually Herman said, "Judge, we're missing…the Defense attorney." Someone had to go out and find him. I think he was in the bathroom having a drink.

After the coroner was Officer Kenneth Leary, a firearms expert. He talked about how each gun produces a unique mark on the bullets that go through its barrel. These are called striation marks, and like fingerprints no two markings are the same. According to this individual, two of the bullets found in Murray Barnes came from the same gun, the third was too broken up for him to identify. This all sounded professional but was irrelevant, since they never found a gun. Another issue Oberfell should have made a big deal about.

Next Officer Len Major took the stand. He was a police officer in the 5th District and one of the first officers on the scene, although he really didn't do anything but turn the case over to Kaufman, who showed up an hour or two later. And Kaufman was next on the stand. He went through the whole chain of events again. When he showed up on the scene, how he brought Freddie Thompson in, and how Thompson fingered me in the lineup.

"Was there any hesitation at all when he positively identified Dan Bright?" Herman asked Kaufman.

"No," Kaufman said. "There was not."

"Did you force or coerce him in any way to pick out that individual?"

"Absolutely not, no."

Herman asked Kaufman how he had gotten the full names of the suspects.

"That was information received pursuant to the investigation that gave us the names of three alleged perpetrators, that being Dan Bright, Christina Davis, and Joseph Brown," Kaufman responded. He was again referring to the bullshit anonymous call.

One issue was that at the hearing in August, Kaufman said he hadn't shown Kevin Singleton a photo lineup. But Kevin had said he was shown a photo lineup. When Oberfell cross-examined Kaufman he asked about this. Kaufman explained that Kevin Singleton *was* shown the photo lineup, but it was at the DA's office, not his own office. And that it was not him who showed the lineup. This was Kaufman's shady way of covering up his earlier lie. Kaufman also played down the fact that Singleton couldn't make an identification. He said he already knew from the initial investigation that Singleton was unable to identify anyone and that he had only later been shown a photo lineup out of "an abundance of caution."

Kaufman repeated Freddie Thompson's description of the shooter as being 5'6, 5'7, light-skinned, wearing a gray sweat suit with a hood. But he said nothing about the shooter having glasses or a mustache. I always have my glasses on, and at that time, I had my mustache. How could this clown remember all these other features and not remember the two most striking ones, whether or not I had any facial hair and whether or not I was wearing glasses? My lawyer should have pressed Thompson on this.

My lawyer also should have asked Kaufman about the two real killers, but he didn't. After the murder, both of them left town, and when they realized someone had been arrested, they came back. But when they found out who I was, they left town again. Herman tried to show that the reason other witnesses didn't come forward was out of fear of retaliation from me. But the real reason no one came forward was because they were scared of the real killers, who were still on the loose.

I wasn't sitting around waiting for these guys to come and take this murder charge for me. I wasn't that stupid. And I wasn't going to tell the police who they were or where to find them. It wasn't my job to do their job for them. My job was to clear my own name. Still a good lawyer would have found the real killers, and they would have found the gun, and they would have pinned the gun to one of them. Of course I had the furthest thing from a good lawyer.

Oberfell spoke real softly, like he was shy or something. Waldron kept asking him to speak up because people were having trouble hearing him. But alcoholics will do that. You can't fully comprehend them. They trail off and mumble. Throughout the trial, Oberfell kept popping all these Life Savers in his mouth. Once he asked me if I wanted one. I looked at him real hard, "Do you know what's going on, man?"

After Kaufman the state called Freddie Thompson to the stand. At first I actually forgot who he was. Why'd they pull a bum off the street and suddenly put him on the stand? Then I remembered. This was the state's star eyewitness, and only eyewitness, and he had supposedly seen me do the crime. As he was repeating his lies to the jury, the state pulled another trick. The fire marshal came into the courtroom and told the judge they had received a bomb threat.

"Escort Mr. Bright to the back," the Judge said, "and do it quietly and speedily."

About six deputies brought me to the back of the courtroom. The judge told everyone else to exit through the side door. The jury wasn't supposed to have contact with anyone during the trial, but as they were escorted from the building, Kaufman and the prosecutors were waiting outside. They told the jury all sorts of stories about me, and that I was under investigation by the FBI for drugs and murders. "After the trial," they said, "you all can come to the DA's office, and we will show you everything."

Because my drug stuff wasn't related to the crime, the DA couldn't bring that up in court. This is one of the reasons why I think they called the bomb threat. They wanted to explain all of this to the jury outside of the courtroom and off the record. I believe the other reason for the bomb threat was to scare the jury into thinking I was so powerful that I could actually place a bomb in a government building. The bomb threat should have been grounds for a mistrial, but my lawyer, being the incompetent alcoholic that he was, didn't do anything. I don't know, because they took me out, but from what I heard, the police and fire department searched the building and found nothing, then they let everyone back in. I do know that jury reentered that courtroom with hate in their eyes.

One question I still have regarding the bomb threat, if I had so much street power that I could arrange to bomb a federal building from prison, why would I rob a bum for $500? Even in the courtroom I had on $800 shoes. And speaking about the money, the killers never even took it. When the shooter pulled his gun out, Barnes ran, and these idiots shot him in the back then ran away. Barnes limped back to the bar to call for help, but where was the money?

There were two $500 envelopes and the police only recovered one, with $444.48 in it. Before he was shot, Barnes bought a round of drinks and gave the bartender a tip, so that explains the missing money in that envelope. But where was the other envelope? Either Freddie Thompson took it himself, or the police took it. Later Jerry Reed, an investigator with the Orleans Indigent Defender Program, went back to the neighborhood to interview people and learned that someone had seen the police take the money. That would not surprise me.

After the bomb threat, Freddie Thompson went back on the stand. Herman asked him to describe how he identified me in the photo lineup. Then, just for dramatic effect, she asked him if he could, "identify the person that you saw in those pictures, the person that you saw in that gray sweat suit, the person that you saw with that gun, are you able to identify him in court today?"

"Yes," Thompson said.

"Can you please point out and describe what he's wearing?" Herman asked.

"I—I don't know what kind of shirt that is he have on…look like black pants, and I don't even know the color of his shirt. I can't make out the color of the shirt."

"It's a button-down shirt?" Herman said, helping him out.

"Yes," Thompson said.

My question is, if this guy can't even identify what kind of clothes I am wearing in a well-lit courtroom when he is sober—maybe sober—how can he identify me late at night with no streetlights when he is drunk?

But Herman was slick. Thompson was a wino and a bum, but she made him into a hero. She didn't give the jury too much time to think about his mumbling ass and quickly brought out Christina Davis, who was in a prison jumpsuit and shackles. She asked Thompson if he could identify her. The real point of this was to parade Christina around in these chains and make her look like a criminal in front of the jury and make it look like I was connected to this criminal individual. Yet another reason for a mistrial.

One thing Herman didn't go into detail about with Thompson was just how drunk he was the night of the murder. But when Oberfell cross-examined Thompson, he actually pressed him on this issue.

"What time on that Sunday did you start drinking?" Oberfell asked Thompson.

"I don't know what time it was," he replied.

"Around lunch time?" Oberfell asked.

"Maybe," Thompson said.

"Maybe a little earlier?"

"Might have been."

"Okay. So is it fair to say that by the time midnight rolled around, you had been drinking steady pretty much all day; is that correct?"

Thompson said yes.

Oberfell had just gotten the state's star witness, the only witness linking me to the crime, to admit that he had been drinking for twelve hours straight the night of the murder!

"So you did not see a mustache," Oberfell continued, "is that correct?"

"No," Thompson said. "I didn't."

"And you didn't see glasses; is that correct?"

"No."

"So, light skinned, five-six or so and a gray sweat-suit—that's all you saw?"

"Yeah."

"You think you would have remembered if the man had glasses and a mustache?"

"Yes, I would have remembered."

But if he could have remembered, and I was the one who did this crime, why didn't he remember?

Oberfell showed Thompson a photo of the bar next door to Creola's. It was shut down and dark and near where Murray Barnes had parked his truck.

"I noticed here there's some light things here, but there's no bulbs in it," said Oberfell. "There were no lights on down there were there?"

"No."

Oberfell was doing alright. He had made the state's star witness look like a drunk fool who witnessed the crime in the dark—exactly what happened—but instead of hammering away at this guy for hours and taking apart his entire story piece by piece, he said, "I have no further questions."

"That's all you have!?" I asked him. "The state's only witness and that's all you're going to ask?"

"I know what I'm doing," he said.

Oberfell should have gone further. He should have asked Thompson about the manner in which Kaufman showed him the photo lineup, and if Kaufman had tapped the photo or signaled me out in any special way. Also Thompson, being the moron he was, was still on parole for a burglary crime he had done back in the early '80s, and by being drunk the night of the murder, he was violating his parole. Oberfell didn't even know that because he hadn't done his homework on Thompson. But he should have known, and he should have pressed Thompson to see if he had been given a deal by the state to ignore the parole violation in order for testifying. Instead he left all of this unsaid.

Even though Oberfell had made Thompson look like a drunk fool, this drunk fool was backed by the government. And this jury was going to believe whatever the government told them to believe. They were not going to trust my shabby-ass lawyer. Every now and then, I glanced over at the jury, just to see what was going on. The black guy was sleeping, and the pregnant woman wasn't paying attention at all. None of them were really paying attention.

"There will be one last witness before lunch," Waldron announced to the jurors, "and then the attorneys have advised me they'll finish the case shortly after lunch this afternoon for you. Thank you again." Once again here was our judge reminding the jury that this capital murder trial, which had begun that morning, would be over shortly after lunch.

That one last witness before lunch was Kevin Singleton. He told Oberfell he couldn't make out who the shooter was because "it was pretty dark," and it all happened too quickly, "in less than two seconds."

"Now, after the shooting took place, did the two guys go down and take anything out of the pockets or anything?" Oberfell asked.

"No," Singleton said.

"What did they do after the shooting happened; they just ran off?"

"They turned around and ran off."

"So it didn't look like a robbery to you, did it?"

"No."

"I'm going to object to that, your Honor," Herman said.

"I'll overrule that," the Judge said.

"And you don't recognize this man here, do you?" Oberfell said, pointing at me.

"No, I don't know him."

This man was at the shooting, had said it was too dark to see clearly, that there was no robbery, and was completely unable to identify me. My lawyer should have immediately made a motion for a mistrial. Instead we broke for lunch. And the judge couldn't help himself but remind the jury one more time that this trial was pretty much already over.

"Ladies of our jury, gentleman of our jury," said Judge Waldron. "Hopefully to enjoy your lunch, please retire to the jury room. Again, as we've stated, the attorneys feel when you return they should be able to start to complete the trial and be finished sometime shortly or early this afternoon."

Every time he said that I would just look at him like, how do you know!? How do you know how long this trial is going to take!? The whole first part of the trial, Waldron never looked at me. He just stared at the clock and counted the minutes going by. He kind of zoned out to that clock, as if he was hoping to speed up time and have the case just be over with. And now this judge was again letting the jury know that the case was almost over, that there was not much to discuss here, and we'd all soon be done and on our way. On to more important things. Meanwhile a man's life was on the line.

CHAPTER TWELVE

THE TRIAL, AFTER LUNCH

By this point, Shelita was sick with lupus, though trying to keep it under control. The steroids would swell
her up, but if she didn't take them, the lupus attacked
her. You could see that she wasn't in the right frame of
mind. This was one strike against her when she took
the stand, the first of my two witnesses. The other
strike was that Oberfell hadn't rehearsed anything
with her.

Oberfell asked Shelita what her relationship with
me was.

"I have two kids by him," she said.

"And are you two planning on getting married?"

"Yes, we are."

Tyra was burning up. But too much was happening
right then for me to worry about that. I was fighting
for my life, and things were going downhill. I was
really starting to think this guy got his license out of

a crackerjack box. For some strange reason, I still believed once the jury heard the real evidence they were going to do the right thing. That didn't happen. Herman cross-examined Shelita, and she tore her apart.

"Miss Christmas," Herman continued. "Do you have any convictions?"

"I have," Shelita said.

"Is that for possession with intent to distribute 31 bags of crack cocaine?"

"Well, they plotted it on me."

"The police officers put these drugs on you?"

"Yes."

"Now, from what I recall, the facts of that case, Miss Christmas, there was a large surveillance of a residence on Desire Street, and you were observed selling crack cocaine to an undercover police officer, and subsequent to your arrest, incident to your arrest, Detective Joseph Thomas searched you…April 18th of 1994, the residence was 2624 Congress Street, and you were observed by Narcotics detectives after a lengthy surveillance, having sold twice to an undercover police officer. After they sold these drugs to you, they placed you under arrest. You struggled and refused to be searched incident to your arrest. You had to be bodily restrained by two Narcotics detectives, at which time Detective Joseph Thomas went into your pocket and retrieved 31 individually wrapped bags of cocaine. The weight of that cocaine, Miss Christmas, ended up being 36.88 grams of cocaine. Do you remember pleading guilty to that charge?"

"Yes, I did," Shelita said.

But Herman wouldn't let her try and tell her version of the story. She did exactly what Oberfell should have done to Thompson. She destroyed her credibility.

I had no emotion. I was still shocked the nightmare had gone this far. When Yam took the stand, Herman did the same thing with him. Yam had a conviction literally from the 1950s, and about twenty years back, he had been arrested for possession of a weapon. About a year ago, he had been arrested for possession of heroin with the intent to distribute, but he hadn't been convicted. Really, Yam hadn't had a conviction for two decades, but Herman made him look like a common thug. And Thompson was an angel.

Oberfell's closing argument for the trial portion wasn't bad. He went through all the state's witnesses and pointed out there was not one shred of physical evidence connecting me to the crime. "Ladies and gentleman," he said, "the only evidence they have, the only evidence out of all of this is the word of that one man who admitted to be drinking all day and all night. And it doesn't even match—Dan doesn't even match the description that he gave that night. That is their whole case."

I think Oberfell probably wanted to make his performance stronger for the record, so higher courts and the public could see that he was doing his job after all, that he was fighting. Although all you have to do is read the transcript and see his overall performance was terrible. Even his closing speech was only about five minutes long. But man, it pissed Karen Herman off.

"Mr. Thompson, could you stand up, please?" she said, in her rebuttal. "Stand up." She was trying to downplay the fact that the person Freddie Thompson described looked nothing like me.

"Look at the complexion of Mr. Thompson," she said, addressing the jury. "Is he dark skinned? Would you say he's a dark-skinned black male? In comparison to him," she said, pointing at me, "is he a light-skinned black male? You compare someone to yourself. Thank you, Mr. Thompson. That's what you do."

She was real flustered and rambled on. "When I see someone with freckles and red hair, I say they're fair-skinned. I tan easily, but I have freckles and red hair. But that person would be fair-skinned. I am a Caucasian female. Am I going to be able to describe an African-American male based on complexions? I'd probably go between dark-skinned and light-skinned. You compare it based on yourself. He's sitting on the passenger seat of a pickup truck. He is looking out of a window, and he sees somebody standing there. He misses the description by three inches? Give me a break. Is that reasonable that that would be a bad I.D. because he says five six or five seven and he's five ten? Six five I'd understand, but five ten? I don't think so."

I wanted to pull her heart out of her chest. She was so good at conniving, so good at misleading. Herman was a real professional. I could see the evilness in her face. She went on for several minutes and finished by pounding her lies into the jury one more time.

"It's first-degree murder. There's absolutely no two ways about it. I had to prove it was him. I had to prove he had the specific intent to do it, and I had to prove it was during the perpetration of an armed robbery or an attempted armed robbery. It's no less if it's an attempt. It's him. There's absolutely no doubt about it. And I would ask you to come back guilty as charged. Thank you."

The old black man finally woke up, the pregnant woman stirred, and the New Orleans Police Department employee was smirking. The jury went into the jury room to deliberate. Less than two hours later, they returned with the verdict. Miss Norman, being the foreperson, presented the verdict sheet to the judge, who read aloud,

"On July 2nd of 1996, we, the jury, find the defendant, Dan L. Bright, guilty as charged, guilty of first-degree murder..."

I sat there in shock. They had found me guilty on the word of a bum. Oberfell told me he was going to file an appeal.

"I don't want you to file shit," I said.

I turned around to look at my family. Everyone was crying. The next morning, I came back for the sentencing. Oberfell had on the same raggedy-baggedy suit and his scarred up black penny loafers. He had alcohol on his breath, and you could smell it on his clothes and skin, too. He was probably out all night drinking. He was a mess, like he was the one on trial facing the death penalty. Again he waived his opening argument. As for Herman, her true pit bull self was out in full force.

"I'm just going to let the evidence speak for itself," she told the jury, "and I'm going to ask you to come back with the only just verdict in this case, and that's death by lethal injection."

As I was sitting there, I found myself wondering, why was Herman so eager in going after the death penalty? This was just your average random black-on-black inner city murder. It happens every night in this city. For most street murder cases, the penalty will be life imprisonment, so why the death penalty for me? I really don't know the answer, but I think the order had to come from up top. And I'm thinking, because they knew she was a pit bull and cared so much about winning, they figured she was the perfect prosecutor for this case.

The DA put the victim's family on the stand. I think it was Murray Barnes's uncle and aunt who spoke. Murray's mother was supposed to take the stand, but they said she had been incapacitated. This was all a tactic. Instead they had the mother sit in the courtroom as Herman asked the aunt and uncle about Murray.

"He didn't drink, he didn't smoke," said the aunt. "And he got along with everyone."

I just stopped paying attention. I blocked it all out. So they decide to give me the death penalty or life, what did it matter? They had already rigged the trial and convicted me.

When the uncle was on the stand, Herman showed him a picture of Murray's family: his mother and all his brothers and sisters. Then Herman looked at the audience and asked the people in the picture to stand up. The DA had coached them all on when to faint, and that photograph was the signal. Murray's mother fell out and started screaming. And I think one of his sisters fainted, too. Herman made sure to make a real big deal of it. "Let the record reflect," she said, "that one of the spectators in the audience appears to have fainted."

And they didn't just faint once, they kept fainting, like three or four times. The whole family was fainting and hollering and screaming and crying. The jury watched all of this, and they were influenced by it. It was a huge disruption, and the judge should have put a stop to it, but he didn't. I just sat there shaking my head. I was starting to hate them all. Fuck Murray Barnes, and fuck his family, fuck the DA, and fuck the judge. Excuse my language, but that's what I was feeling.

Oberfell wanted to put my mother and sister on the stand, but I didn't want to give the state the satisfaction of watching my family beg for my life. It was a legal war, and I had lost. I wanted to take my lick and go.

"I suggest you let your mother get on the stand for you," the judge told me off the record.

My sister listened to me, but my mother didn't listen. She decided to go up there anyway. I stood up to block her path, but she pushed me aside.

"This is my first time sitting in a chair like this," said my mother. "I just want to say I love my son. I know those people love their son and their brother and all of this. I lost a son in '94 in my arms with 11 bullets in front my door. I know what they feel. It's not like I don't hurt for them. I hurt for my child, too. I still hurt for him. I held him in my arms when he died, and I look out that window every day and see where he laid. I know what those people are going through.

I'm just asking y'all to let me be able to go see my only son that's left. That's all. He got four children, little children outside in the hall. I'm just asking just make it, so I can just go see the only son I got left…"

After about two minutes, I motioned to my little sister to get her off the stand. I think my mother knew how upset I was.

"That's all I have to say," she continued. "That's all I can say. That's all I know to say, what's in my heart. That's it. That's it. Please let me go, go see about my grandbabies in the hall."

Herman's assistant gave a closing argument then Oberfell spoke. He was mumbling, and the judge had to ask him to speak up and take his time.

"Murray Barnes is murdered," said Oberfell. "He's gone. Dan's brother was murdered. There's just too many murders happening in this city. The killing has to stop. The killing has to stop. But what I say to you is this: What if it turns out in the future that Freddie Thompson made a mistake? What if he made a mistake? If you sentence Dan to death, we can't correct that mistake. If you sentence him to life, that mistake can always be corrected. Death is so final. Are we so sure that we are ready to take a life this morning? Are we so sure? Thank you."

I later found out this might have been the shortest closing argument for a murder case in Louisiana history. Herman then had one more chance to dig the knife in even further, which she gladly used. "You found him guilty as charged yesterday," she said. "You know he did it. You know he had a specific intent to kill while he was committing an armed robbery or an attempted armed robbery…It's time for him to take responsibility for his actions. An eye for an eye, ladies and gentlemen. That's what I'm asking for. That's what it boils down to…He deserves to die."

The jury was adjourned to deliberate and eat lunch. When they returned, the judge asked me to rise so the verdict could be read. I turned my back. I wouldn't face them. It was a sign of disrespect to the jury and the judge and DA. I didn't approve of what they had done. They hadn't shown me any type of respect. They didn't even weigh the evidence out. I wanted to show them that I didn't approve of their verdict and how they had treated me. The judge just looked at me, and I think Oberfell told me it would be more respectful if I turned and faced him.

So I turned back around, and the judge read, "The jury determines that the defendant be sentenced to death." I was 27 years old.

I looked at my family, they were all crying. Even the policewoman I had been having sex with was crying. As the policeman walked me back to my tier, he whispered, "They railroaded you, everyone in there saw that. And your lawyer was with them."

I looked at him and said nothing. When I got back to my tier, Manny told me he had some food for me. I told him I didn't want it.

"What happened?" he asked.

Everybody in OPP thought I was going to beat that charge. I just put my thumb down and kept walking. He asked again. He didn't believe me.

"The death penalty," I said. "That's what happened, they gave me the fucking death penalty."

Later that night, visitation started. Shelita came first. I told her to go on with her life. I didn't want her wasting her last days running around for me, running to the court building, the jailhouse, keeping on the lawyers. I just wanted her to enjoy the little time she had left without worrying about me. She started crying. She knew she was going to die. In fact she knew more than she was telling people. The doctors had given her a month to live.

Shelita made my mother promise to take care of the twins and raise them herself. That was the most important thing she wanted settled before she died. Her own mother wanted nothing to do with the twins because of me. Shelita also knew that her family would misuse and mistreat them. My mother was just happy to have the kids.

Later Tyra visited. I asked her if she was alright because she didn't look alright. Her eyes were puffy and red. Her hair wasn't combed. She had it in a ponytail.

"I'm alright," she said.

"I don't know how long I am going to be in this hell hole," I told her. "You are young and beautiful. You need to go on with your life."

Tyra was not the type to go to war with you. She was about family. And I just wanted her to be happy. But she didn't want to hear any of that. She said she wanted to stay together, that she would stick by my side. She didn't care how long it was going to be.

"I knew what I was getting into when we got together!" she cried. "I'm going all the way with you."

So I gave her the rules. I said it is going to be long. I don't care about you having a man or boyfriend on the side, just find someone who doesn't know me and make sure he is not in the same business as me. Find a guy a little older than me, not one of these young guys. And tell me about it. Don't hide some relationship behind my back.

Tyra said she didn't care about any of that. She convinced me that she wanted to stick it out with me.

I think it was a few weeks after the trial ended that I called home one night to talk to my son.

"I have something to tell you," said Tyra.

"What's the bad news this time?"

"I don't know how to tell you."

"Just say it and get it over with," I told her.

"Your grandmother is dead."

I didn't say anything for about five minutes.

"Are you alright?" she asked.

"How did she die?"

"She had a heart attack…she has been dead for about a week. No one wanted to tell you, they wanted me to do it, but I didn't know how."

I thought about all the big Thanksgiving and Christmas parties at my grandmother's house, how we had both loved custard pie, and she had always gotten custard pies at the bakery just for us and wouldn't let anyone else touch them. I thought about the times I took her to bingo. I thought about how she always defended me.

My grandmother hadn't come to the trial. She couldn't handle me being locked up, shackled up, chained up. She would call my mother or aunt every thirty minutes to ask what was going on though. When I first got arrested, she started to get sick. My grandmother had always been kind of sick, but she was healthy, too. She had kept going to church and bingo but hearing the news about me affected her. It was a surprise when Tyra told me, at the same time I knew it was going to happen. Now she had peace. But I missed my grandmother, my friend.

Before going to Angola, I had one more chance, with Gary Bailey, who filed a motion for a new trial. He was a real player-type lawyer, and one of our street lawyers. I had been worried about using him at first because he was connected to me, but now I didn't care. I needed his help.

Bailey liked going against the system. In his office, there was a big picture of a marijuana plant. He sent an investigator into the neighborhood near Creola's, and this guy said that everyone he spoke with said I was innocent. Two new witnesses even came forward. But it didn't work. This judge wasn't budging. He wanted to wrap things up as quickly as possible because, he told the court, he had to get ready for a New Year's party. I was given an execution date, to die by lethal injection, on March 15, 1997.

This wasn't a real date, it could be appealed, but it was still frightening to have your death date written down on paper. But I wasn't going to lay down in the fetal position and start crying. If they planned to execute me, I planned to fight until the end. It was right around Christmas. In the parish jail, they don't do a damn thing for Christmas, it's the same routine. They are big on this processed turkey, this strange white meat stuff. White, man, white, white, white. And they put it with beans. I was thinking they weren't going to move me to Angola until after the New Year. But on December 27th, 1996, the police came to my tier.

"Let's go, Mr. Bright," they said, "we have a long trip ahead of us."

CHAPTER THIRTEEN

ANGOLA

Angola used to be a slave plantation, and during much of the 1900s, it was the bloodiest and most violent prison in America. Corrupt racist guards, knife fights every day, guys getting raped, prisoners buying and selling other prisoners for sex, filthy medieval conditions. In 1995, right about the time I was put on Death Row, a short pudgy country boy named Burl Cain became Warden. Cain looks like the Penguin from Batman. In the city, he'd be a fish out of water, some goofy redneck with a cowboy hat, but he ruled Angola. The prison became his home. By using God and labor, he cleaned it up, though what he really did was brainwash people with Christianity. He made prisoners into tools for profit and tools for entertainment. Visit Angola today and you'd think you were stepping back into slavery days.

Cain uses religion to humble the convicts. When you humble someone, they are no longer a threat to you, which leaves you free to do what you want with them. At a zoo, how can you tell the difference between the animal bred in captivity and the animal captured in the wild? The wild animal has a certain look in his eye. He's always trying to figure a way out. And Burl Cain is trying to figure a way to kill that wild instinct. When you humble someone, they forget about their fight, their struggle, their freedom. They give in, and after a while, that look in their eye becomes dimmer. It goes away. They become programmed, they have been institutionalized, and they accept anything Burl Cain says to them. And then Cain can get to what he's really about: money.

Angola is a multimillion-dollar business. The mattresses and pillows you see in prisons all across America are made at Angola factories. There is a tag plant that produces Louisiana license plates. You got the metal fab, a silkscreen shop, where they make badges and highway signs. They also make prison jackets and prison soap for the whole Louisiana prison system. There's a print shop, a broom and mop factory, and a body and fender shop, where police bring their wrecked cars and convicts fix them up. They make dog food, too. They got all these different barrels of breads and beans and rice, and they grind it together and send it to a regular dog food factory—dog food rich people's pets are eating is probably made in some prison. They also make their own brand of hot sauce called Guts & Glory. And they fix wheelchairs and ship them to Third World countries. And the prisoners make coffins. Their own coffins.

But the largest operation is farming. Angola is almost as big as Manhattan and located in a big old bend in the Mississippi River. It covers some of the richest farmland in the South. They grow cotton and wheat and all sorts of vegetables: corn, soybeans, cabbage, onions, okra, peppers, squash, tomatoes. They have a strawberry patch and a fishpond, and they have thousands of beef cows, and they have bulls and horses. Nice horses. Prisoners raise them, and then Cain sells them to police departments, including the New Orleans Police Department. The police horses tourists see trotting down Bourbon Street were brought up by prisoners at Angola.

Burl Cain likes doing things the old fashioned way, with hard labor. For cash crops, Cain uses tractors and modern equipment because he wants the money faster, but when it comes to crops like okra and peas, he would rather have inmates pick them by hand, not just to break the inmates but to have something for us to do. Prisoners work in the field eight hours a day, five days a week. Pay starts at two cents an hour. And for trustees, guys who have earned their working privileges, pay tops out at 20 cents an hour. That's considered a good wage at Angola.

Break someone down then put them back up with religion, that's Cain's way. It's a psychological tactic. Out in the fields, guards sit on these big old horses, with shotguns and carbine rifles. Another guard rides up and down the field with a pistol, making sure everyone stays in line. When you come out of the field, the only thing you have a chance to do is church. There are different social clubs, but they are really all church clubs. You can get a degree, the only degree offered at a Louisiana prison, but it's with the Baptist church. Everything is church. Church, church, church.

Angola has two cemeteries, with graves dug by the prisoners. There is also a golf course, built by prisoners. And there's a radio station called *The kicks behind the bricks*. At first it was a good station, then it started playing all types of gospel. It became just another way for Burl Cain to brainwash people, to get his message out. He is on the radio more than the music, talking about prison reform, prison improvements, how the violence is down. Every time you turn on the radio, he's there, with this light scraggly, old whiney voice.

At the entrance to Angola, there's a museum with old knives prisoners once tried to juke people with and a rusty old electric chair the prison used to kill people with. They've got zipguns, which is a prison gun, and shanks, any old weapon that convicts used to hurt one another. For instance, they had a guy before my time who made a gun out of paper, with a real bullet. The gun had a paperclip, and when it broke, it made the back of the bullet explode. You only got one shot with that gun, then it caught fire.

The museum dates back to the 1950s and makes Burl Cain look good because as bad as things are now, they are better than they were then. In fact they've got a whole section of the museum dedicated to Burl Cain. Books about Burl Cain, awards for Burl Cain, Burl Cain standing beside a pair of giant alligators hanging by their necks from ropes, Burl Cain's face on a coffee mug. They even got a Coke with his name printed on it. The museum also has a gift shop, where they sell coffee mugs and tote bags and souvenirs related to the Angola rodeo.

The rodeo takes place in a stadium built by inmates. What they make these guys do is ridiculous, modern-day Roman gladiator shit. There are a number of games. In one, four guys sit at a card table playing poker, and a bull comes crashing through. Whoever is the last one to stay sitting down wins. They call that "Convict Poker." Another game is "Guts and Glory." They hang a $100 check off the horn of a bull, and inmates try to grab it. In another game, convicts dress like clowns and get in a rubber barrel while the bull tries to hit them up in the air. I don't know the exact rules to that game, but I think the object is to see who can stay in the barrel the longest. The rodeo has all different types of slavery entertainment.

There is regular old bull riding, too. Throw some guy with no training on a bull, and the bull tries to shake them off. Right before the rodeo, they are supposed to train you, but someone told me they don't, they just throw you out there. Apparently you sign an agreement saying you can't sue if something happens. Then someone pins a number on your shirt and out you go. A lot of the time, guys get seriously wounded. Sometimes there are fatalities, guys who don't make it.

You have to remember, these bulls can weigh more than a ton. And a lot of these prisoners are from the inner city, they aren't used to riding no bulls around. Most people won't tell you why the bulls get so wild and crazy. I've heard it is because they tie their testicles down and shock them. So the bull is already bucking, and it's pissed off because someone tied a rope around his testicles. Now you got this poor convict trying to hang onto the thing. And the crowd goes nuts, wanting blood. All of this is just to amuse the warden and his redneck hillbilly friends. It's a sport for these rich folks to watch and laugh at, a blood sport.

Everything I am describing happens at Angola, but it happens in what they call general population. I had done some time in general population at Angola before, about 18 months on drug charges, and so I knew a good bit about what went on there. But death row was its own world. We didn't participate in the rodeo, we didn't go out into the fields, we didn't work in the factories. Our world was our tier, a long hallway with cells on one side and at the head, a shower, an exercise bar, and a phone. In the hallway, there was a TV, and there were windows so we could see when it was light and dark, day and night. Every day you had an hour to shower, use the phone, do your exercises, and walk up and down the hall and stretch your legs. Three days a week, we had an hour on the yard, each of us in our own little pen. The guys played a sort of death row football. With a bunch of socks they made a ball and threw it to each other over the fences that separated the pens. If a guy was in a middle pen, he would try to catch the ball out of the air.

At first, time went slow. I'd catch myself looking through the bars and out the window. I couldn't see trees, just sky. I wondered what was happening back in the city, what my son was doing, my daughters were doing, Shelita and Tyra, my mother. For a week, I didn't do much more than sit on my bed and think. But that's the wrong way to go about prison time. You have to do the time, not let the time do you. You have to entertain your mind because if you don't, your mind will entertain you, and you don't want that. That's when you start seeing the wall moving and paint falling off.

Still I stuck to myself. Or at least, I tried to. One day I was out on the tier for my hour and heard: "You alright down there? Need something to eat or drink?"

"No, I'm cool," I said.

This was Big Phil, in the next cell over—Bird was on the other side of me. Big Phil was about 6'4 or 6'5, 250 pounds. We spoke for a bit, and I found out we were both from the 9th Ward.

"I know who you are," he said. "If you need something, man, don't let your deputy stop you from asking. I have some tapes and some magazines, *Playboys*, *Black Tails*..."

"Maybe later," I told him.

"We are hooking up later," said Big Phil. "I'll send you down some."

"Hooking up what?" I asked.

"Times up," said the guard, and walked me back to my cell.

The next day, I met Magic, on the other side of Big Phil. Magic was a small guy, like 5'5, and from the Westbank, across the river from New Orleans.

I soon found out that hooking up meant making dinner for each other. Let's say they served fried chicken for dinner. If I was hooking up that night, I'd get everyone's chicken, tear it up, and make a chicken salad. You might have soup, too, and you mix some of that in. Then people took whatever stuff they had from the canteen: meat, cheese, chips, pickles, tuna fish and passed it my way. I hooked all that up and made a casserole, and I gave the food to the guards, or somebody who was on their hour—somebody who was trustworthy, not some psychopath. They put it in the microwave, which was at the front of the tier then brought it back. Now I used tissue paper and wrapped up sandwiches and passed them down, and there you go, you had a nice meal. Big Phil, Magic, and I hooked up almost every single night.

Come 8 or 9 at night, the tier was real quiet and peaceful. Sometimes it was so quiet it was spooky, you could hear your watch ticking. I usually read. We had a book list and were allowed five books a week. That jail cell was like my think tank. The first thing I read was *Black's Law Dictionary*. I didn't want to be ignorant of the law anymore, and I never wanted to be taken advantage of again. I realized that the law was actually composed of simple words, but lawyers just spent most of their time trying to confuse people. I read everything there was to read, even if it was about an ant. But mostly I read and reread a certain set of books: *The Art of War, War and Peace, The 48 Laws of Power,* the Bible, the Koran, the Criminal Code and Procedure, the Constitution. If you could master these books, you were a dangerous man. Even police would fear you because you knew the law, and you had knowledge.

We had one guy on the tier we called Bird. This man never picked up a book. All Bird did was watch TV, all day long. Never did anything to help himself, never called his lawyers. Bird was there because he was young and stupid. Him and five other guys juked up an old white woman to get in a gang, and all six got charged with murder. The other five were in general population, the regular part of the prison, but Bird got death row. He was from Alexandria, this little city out in the country. I once asked Bird where he stayed at, and he said a trailer. I was like, "A trailer!" I didn't even know black people stayed in trailers. I thought those were worse than the Projects. But trailers were a big thing in the countryside. Some trailers were bigger than houses, although I don't think Bird stayed in any trailer like that.

"Bird, man," I asked, "why don't you ever work on your case?"

"Fuck that," he said. "I don't want to know nothing about my case."

I felt bad for Bird. He had given up on his case, and he wasn't good for books, but if we wanted to know what was going to be on TV, he was the man. "Yo Bird, what's coming on down the line?" one of us would ask, and he'd know. Bird will probably be at Angola watching that TV until the day of his execution.

We had another guy on my tier named John Connelly, this short white guy with sandy brown hair. John was very intelligent and also very sick. He was a Sunday school teacher, and in the back of the church he raped and killed a nine year old boy. That horrible image always stood out in my mind. John was from one of those little bitty Louisiana towns, and he was schizophrenic. Sometimes he'd be bright and talkative. He told these highly intelligent jokes, not your average jokes. When he was alright, he was real good people; if you needed something he gave it to you. But John flipped real quick. He was an awkward guy, and he wasn't right in the head. In the back of the church, man, he beat the kid, molested him, and raped him.

We had another guy named Michael Owen Perry. He was mentally challenged, although I don't know if Mike was really crazy or just acted like it. He defecated all over the tier, defecated in the shower. Every so often, guards came in there and tear gassed him down or beat him. But Mike had another side, too. If we were having an intellectual conversation, Mike would be deep into it with us. Or, say you were writing a letter and needed someone to spell a word, Mike was your guy. Afterward, though, he'd start cursing and yelling at you, "Stop fucking with me!" People like Mike went from zero to a hundred in a split second, good to evil, and when they went to evil, they could do evil shit. This was a new type of individual for me. In New Orleans, we had shooting and drugs and street crime. On death row we had guys like John and Mike.

If I'm not mistaken, Mike killed his sister, his mother, his father, and also an infant nephew. From what I heard, his sister was mentally handicapped, too. He used to have sex with her. He had a list of other targets. He was going to kill the Australian singer Olivia Newton-John, and when they arrested him, he

was on his way to the Supreme Court to kill Justice
Sandra Day O'Connor. The Supreme Court case Ford v.
Wainwright established that a mentally insane person
cannot be executed, but the state pulled a trick with
Mike. When he was on medication, they claimed he
wasn't insane. So as long as Mike was kept on medication, he was considered mentally competent and could
be executed. Mike tried to refuse his medications, and
the state forced him to take them. But the courts ruled
you can't force a man to take medication, that's cruel
and unusual punishment. So, as long as Mike acted
insane, the state couldn't kill him. This made it tough
to tell if Mike was acting crazy just to stay alive or
really crazy. But if he was acting, he deserved an Oscar.

Mike would go two or three weeks without showering. He'd have waste all over his arms, his pants. We'd
tell him to shower and he'd just stand in the shower,
without doing anything then walk up and down the
tier buck-naked. Mike was in the first cell because he
was on suicide watch. The first cell was always reserved
for suicide watch. Sometimes guys messed with Mike,
they'd tell him to do things, like pull his pants down
in front of the police, just to pass the time. Like I said,
there are some twisted people on death row. But Mike
was still part of our family. If we had sandwiches left
over, we sent them his way. We helped him out when
we could. Every family has one of those types, and
Mike was it.

CHAPTER FOURTEEN

LIFE ON DEATH ROW

Angola was like the Walmart of West Feliciana Parish. Everyone worked there. The black workers came from Mississippi, to the north, and had their own entrance into the prison, and the white workers came from Louisiana, to the south, and through the main entrance. For a lot of guards, Angola was their whole world. They had their own communities within the prison, like a little suburb, with houses and stores and their own elementary school. A lot of kids who grew up on Angola went into the military, then came right back to the prison as a higher rank.

You had maybe five big families that controlled Angola, and the men in those families had most of the ranking positions. People worked there whose fathers and grandfathers had worked there. These kids grew up watching men get shackled, men made to fall in line, men made to work for nothing out in those hot fields. And these kids became the next generation of guards. So it was not surprising that some of them grew up to be racist redneck motherfuckers.

At one point, one of these Ku Klux Klan motherfuckers who had grown up at Angola came over from general population. He thought death row was going to be like general population, and that he could treat prisoners the same way. It might be time to eat, and the trustees would bring up our food. "You set that food down," he told them. "These black-ass convicts don't need to eat." Once the food was cold, he passed it out.

We called our lawyers, we called death penalty groups, we called the media about this guy. And all kinds of people were calling Burl Cain. If there was one thing this corrupt-ass warden didn't want, it was media attention. To cap it off, we went on a hunger strike. Doctors and human rights people came on death row to make sure we were still alive, and it was all over the news. Burl Cain didn't even transfer this guard. He let him go. Then Cain went to the media and said the problem had been resolved, it was all a misunderstanding.

But soon after, an ignorant black guard came on our tier and was trying to impress the white guards. It didn't matter that he was black, he was from Mississippi and didn't like us. "Chill your ass out," the other guards told him, "you don't know what tier you're on." But he didn't listen. We called our attorneys and filed sexual harassment charges. We said this guy was winking at us in the shower, licking his lips. Cain let him go. Before leaving the guard came to us, crying.

Can you imagine how hard it was going to be for him to find another prison job with a charge on his record of sexual harassing a couple inmates?

"Tell me what you need, and I will get it for you," Cain finally told us. "Just stop calling your lawyers, you all have problems with your deputy, come tell me first!"

So what did we get? Church. A preacher in a black and white suit with a tie used to walk up and down the tier preaching. Now Cain let us use an empty room on the second floor of death row for services. He gave Christian brothers Sunday and Muslim brothers Friday. That's how we got to know people on other tiers. We were still in shackles and handcuffs, and our handcuffs were hooked to big leather restraining belts. But we could talk, and we could kind of lift our hands up and shake hands. If there was someone in a different tier we wanted to speak with we gave a trustee a verbal message to pass along. Or we gave them a letter, what we called a kite. We also had the prison Internet system, hollering through vents. Either way the person got the message and came to the next church service, and we sat together and talked. One person I liked to speak with was Shareef Cousin.

Shareef is one of the youngest people in the history of the United States to be put on death row. He was 16 when they convicted him of murder and sent him to Angola to be executed. The crime involved a white couple who had been eating dinner at Port of Call, a popular restaurant in the French Quarter. As the couple was walking back to their car, the man was robbed and murdered. Because it was the French Quarter, the whole city was watching, and the DA's office needed a conviction. Shareef was playing in a youth basketball game until just minutes before the murder happened.

Everyone knew he was playing basketball. There was a video of him playing basketball, and the two referees from the game both said he was playing basketball. His coach gave testimony, too. The basketball game got started late, and the coach drove Shareef and three other teammates home, and the murder actually happened while he was driving them home. The coach told the prosecutors this, and they recorded him. But the prosecutors recut the tape, making it seem like the game ended earlier than it actually had, and that Shareef was around to do the murder.

That wasn't even the worst thing these criminal prosecutors did in Shareef's case. Those three teammates were going to testify that they were with Shareef at the time of the murder. They showed up at the courthouse the day of the trial, but some people from the DA's office told them the trial wasn't on yet and to come wait in a building across the street. It was a trick. And the teammates were never able to testify.

The police used the same photo lineup tactic they had used in my case. Put six pictures up and tell the witness to "look at this one real good," then tap the one they want picked. The main witness in Shareef's case was the date of the guy who had been killed, but she was nearsighted and wasn't wearing her contact lenses at the time of the murder. At first she went on record saying she couldn't identify the suspect, that without her lenses she could only see "shapes and patterns."

But after this police lineup scam, she suddenly was able to identify Shareef with absolute certainty.

Man, these guys pulled every trick in the book to convict Shareef, to put this child in prison. And not just to put him in jail, to execute him. But somehow, despite all that was done against him, and despite him being just a kid and forced to spend time with murderers and psychopaths, Shareef was always upbeat. He got to death row a few months before me, and when he found out I was up there, he passed word through a trustee that he wanted to see me. I didn't know Shareef personally, but I knew his case. Shareef's case was famous. When we finally met face-to-face, we got along well.

"When I talk to you, I get this energy," Shareef said. He was big on this energy thing. Every person transfered energy to the people around them. You have positive energy and negative energy, and if you are always negative, that energy is going to rub off, if you are positive, that energy rubs off, too. Even though he was so young, Shareef was the one telling me to be strong, and that everything was going to be alright. He just had a good nature about him. With his knowledge and intelligence, he could have been anything he wanted. If he hadn't been convicted at age 16, Shareef would probably be running his own Fortune 500 Company.

Another person I talked to at church was JT, or John Thompson, whose case I already mentioned. JT wasn't much older than Shareef when he first got to death row. They convicted him of murder at age 22. By the time I got up there, JT had already been on death row for a decade. On about eight different occasions, he had been given an execution date. JT wasn't carefree like Shareef. He was embattled because he had these execution dates. A couple times it ran up to just a few days before the execution, then an appeal finally came through. "You all ain't taking this seriously," JT would tell Shareef and I, as we were laughing about something. "These dudes are going to kill us!"

Every case was different, but boiled down they were all the same: corrupt police officers, corrupt prosecutors. Even if you did your crime, you didn't get a fair trial. Police and prosecutors lied and cheated to convict you. If you truly didn't do the crime, they went above and beyond to convict you. They lied and cheated even more. There wasn't anything unusual about being wrongfully convicted in Louisiana.

The only reason people get off is because legal groups like the Capital Assistance Center and the Innocence Project take their case. But what about all the cases these lawyers don't take? What about all the cases that aren't investigated? What about all the non-death row cases? How many innocent people are rotting their lives away at Angola? Most of the people there are serving life sentences. Apparently 90 percent of inmates die there. That's out of a prison population of 6,000 people. How many guys do you think got a fair trial? Do you really think Orleans Parish could act so illegally in a handful of cases, like mine and JT's and Shareef's, but follow the law in all their other cases? You think they were crooked on the death row cases but somehow fair on the petty stuff? Hell no.

During my time on death row, I tried not to get carried away with all of that thinking. I tried to stay calm and focus on my case. I meditated, too. I visualized. I could put myself anywhere in the world. I could tell you the color of sand on beaches in Brazil or Hawaii even though I'd never been there. I saw these beaches perfectly, beautiful clear water, beautiful women walking around with G-strings, me living there in a cottage on the beach. I spent hours there. I went to the Bahamas and Bermuda. I loved going to Monte Carlo. I had a townhouse on Central Park.

I also took road trips. I'd be driving on the interstate in a nice luxury car, a Mercedes or a Bentley, listening to Freddie Jackson, or Luther Vandross, or Phil Collins. I was thinking about business, how to put together multimillion-dollar deals, multibillion-dollar deals. I might drive from New Orleans to California, stop at little towns, have lunch. Maybe I'd stop at Shoney's or Denny's, or some restaurant on the side of the road. A beautiful woman might be working there. Maybe she looked like Halle Berry. She might be struggling to put her way through college, or just struggling, and we might hook up. I'd ask her if there was a hotel in town. Turns out there was a small hotel, and she directed me there. Later she picked me up and showed me around. She told me about her little town. She took me to some of the neighborhood clubs. When I left, I'd give her like ten or twenty thousand dollars. Not for sex, but to help her out. And I might get her number and call her back later to give her more money.

I went days without talking, just visualizing. Guys would knock on the wall.

"You alright over there?"

"Yeah, I'm good," I'd tell them, then go back to the vision in my head.

If I was not traveling the world, I was building my dream house. I built this house over 100 times. It was so beautiful. I could tell you every cut, every corner, every piece of concrete, every piece of marble. The color of the walls, the grass on the lawn, the gym, the indoor pool, the entertainment room, the furniture, the tennis court, the driveway, cameras in the kitchen, cameras throughout the house, fish tanks with sharks in it. This house was locked in my brain, and every week I went back in to add something, to touch up the details.

I tried to do things in my head for designing a house that no one else had done before. I might have an octagon fish tank sitting in the middle of spearmint green marble floors. I might have marble on the floors and walls, or a fish tank that when you look at it, looked like a hole in the floor but was actually a concrete trench filled with goldfish that traveled through the entire house. An elevator connected my room to the library, which had all sorts of books, law books, history books, literature books, business books, everything a real library would have had. The pool had a two-story pool house, and on the top floor were games like pinball, for my kids. And a tunnel, several tunnels actually, so I could leave the library and go to the gym or my indoor pool without leaving the house. And this wasn't some old drippy tunnel, this was a state of the art tunnel.

The house wasn't in New Orleans, it was somewhere like Texas or Lafayette or Opelousas, somewhere with lots of cheap land. I'd have like 50 acres of land so I always had room to add on to the house. I took my time building this house. And I didn't build it with drug money. I was a businessman. I was into real estate, construction, export. I exported used vehicles to South America, something that no one else was really doing. I shipped some to Africa, too, some place where the economy was real shabby, but they had money. Maybe I got a contract with the drug kingpins over there. Maybe I sold them cars or bulletproofed their cars for them. I had other business interests, too. I got government contracts to help rebuild war-torn countries. But everything was legit.

There was no air conditioning on death row. In summertime there was a fan that blew hot air up and down the tier. The temperature was about 110 degrees. In wintertime there was no heat, so you stayed in thermal wear. We had blankets and thick mattresses. The mattresses were cotton, with hard blue plastic wrapped around them, then sheets over that, white sheets and a white bedspread and a pillow. The pillow had the same hard plastic wrapped around. Everything was made at Angola. I put a blanket in the pillowcase, to make it more comfortable. Then I took my clothes and put them at the end of the mattress, to make the mattress come up. That way I could read in bed with my head lifted up.

I read so much I got these headaches, migraines that developed from tension and thinking so hard and also reading in the dark. They turned the lights off at night, and all you had was a dim safety light out in the hallway. It was a little bitty bulb, and they covered it with a blue cap so the light was blue and difficult to see. To read at night you had to get out of bed and sit by the bars and angle your book a certain way to catch the glow. Flashlights were not allowed. I complained about the headaches, but they didn't want to take the chance in bringing me to a doctor.

Everyone who goes to Angola ends up getting sick. I knew a bunch of guys who came up healthy, but when you were there 20, 30, 40 years, you were bound to get sick. There was something in the soil, and it was in the water, too. Angola grew their own vegetables, but these pesticide planes flew over and sprayed chemicals on the food. And while the plane was spraying, guys were out there picking or chopping grass. Another thing, and I'm not sure why, but at Angola everyone's teeth were always falling out. Prisoners told stories about trips to the dentist, some doc standing on your chest and pulling your teeth out. Pieces of tooth getting caught in your gums and staying stuck in there.

Angola had a real hospital with different departments, but you have to remember, these were some messed up docs. These weren't top of the class doctors. These were bottom of the class doctors, the ones who barely made it through medical school, docs who had nowhere else to go so they stuck them in prisons. There are doctors in Louisiana penitentiaries with psychotic disorders. There are doctors who have been found drinking on the job. There are doctors who have been to prison themselves, for selling drugs or using methamphetamines. Doctors who have been to prison for possessing child pornography. And they would't even let me see these clown docs.

Right after I was found guilty, my mother had a series of heart attacks. At first no one told me because they didn't want to upset me. My mom doesn't like discussing her health. You ask her, and she'll say, "I'm alright." I still called my mother at least once a month, but I didn't like calling because I knew it put strain on her. I never talked to my father. He might have been willing to talk, but he didn't know how to talk. It was just uncomfortable.

My mother visited, too. She came all the way up from the city, a three-hour trip, then went all the way back down. They had this bus that went to Angola once or twice or week, and it was filled with people from New Orleans heading up there to visit family members. My mother would come up here and start crying, but at the same time, she saw that I was alright and that made her happy. "Ma, these people can't kill me," I told her. "I know the law now." That made her feel good, but at the same time, she asked, "Why are you still here?"

One morning I came out on the tier for my hour. Phil and Magic were both asleep so I took a shower and called my mother.

"Are you okay?" she asked.

"Yes," I said.

But she asked again, and one moment later, she asked again.

"Why are you asking me the same thing over and over?"

"Baby, didn't you hear?"

"Hear what?"

"Shelita is dead. She passed two days ago."

I don't say anything. Back in my cell, I just sit there on my bed thinking about all the good times Shelita and I had together. I miss her.

Around that same time, things started going bad for me and Tyra. One Saturday she came for a contact visit, with Lil' Man. You might wonder how we got intimate with Lil' Man around, but at that time, Lil' Man was still little. In fact, one time I was sitting there with my hand between Tyra's legs, and Lil' Man said, "Daddy get your hands out of mammy's booty!" He didn't know the difference between front and back, to him the whole area was booty.

Tyra was usually happy and playful but not that day. She wouldn't look me in the eyes. I knew something was up, it was like a piece of her wasn't there. This wasn't the woman I fell in love with. After we were done, I played with Lil' Man, and when the visit was over, I looked at her and smiled, "What's his name, and do I know him?"

"No," she said. She was almost relieved, now she could finally put it out in the open. "And he don't know you, he's a square working man."

"He must live on the fucking moon not to know me," I said.

"I would never fool with anyone who knew you," she said. "And besides, we are just friends."

"Did you have sex with him?" I asked.

She didn't say anything.

"Did you fuck him?!" I asked.

"One time," she said.

It felt like someone had shot me in the chest.

When I got back to my cell, Magic and Phil yelled down the hall, asking me how my visit went. I didn't say anything. I was just so angry. It wasn't about her messing around. It was about her not being honest with me. Instead of her being up front, I had to figure it out on my own.

I know it was hypocritical for me to be mad. When I told my mother, she told me, "Didn't you make her pregnant when you were with this girl or that girl? Didn't you do the same thing to her?" She was right, and as time went on, I accepted it, but I didn't let anyone know I accepted it. I still had a lot of hate for her, and I had too much pride. It was a man thing. I had that tunnel vision. I stopped thinking. My mind became a rage, and because I was locked up in prison, it was especially difficult to control the anger.

I wanted to show Tyra I remained powerful, so I called someone I knew still out on the streets and told them to go over there and burn her car. This guy poured gas all over her vehicle and lit it on fire, a brand new Dodge Neon. Tyra was in denial. She thought the engine had malfunctioned, or there had been an electrical shortage. But when the fire department came, they told her the car was lit on fire. Then it dawned on her who might be behind it. I really just wanted to show her a lesson, that I could still affect her.

For weeks I barely left my cell. I was thinking about it all. It's funny how things worked out. I was trying to figure which woman to leave and which one to keep, and when the smoke cleared, one died and one left me.

One day I learned Lucky had been found guilty. Almost everyone in the case ratted on him. The Feds said they had him under surveillance for over a year before they arrested him. Later that night, I was lying down reading and thinking. I remembered the visit from the Feds while I was on trial. If they had him under surveillance, then they had me under surveillance. I jumped up, excited. For some reason, it hadn't dawned on me before, but sitting there in prison with nothing but time, it finally did. If the Feds had been watching us for a year, they had to have been watching me the night of the murder, which meant they knew I didn't commit this crime.

An inmate counsel named Calvin Duncan helped me fill out the forms so I could file a Freedom of Information Act request to the FBI and obtain my records. Calvin was the go-to man on legal issues, and he was the one who really reached out and helped me learn the law. He told me which law books to get and helped me get case law when a specific case came up in what I was reading. There were some inmate councils you paid in cigarettes, or had people on the outside send money to, so they could work on your case, but Calvin did everything free of charge. He prided himself on that. I don't think Calvin had much family, maybe a sister. He was a real good person, and he had a real good heart. The thing about Calvin, he could help everyone but himself. His case had some com-plexities that made his own exoneration very difficult. Wherever you go in a prison there is someone like Calvin, helping everyone out but can't help himself.

I didn't hear from the FBI for many months. Then I got the letter. They had rejected my request. Calvin and I filed again and again, trying all sorts of tactics to get them to send me my FBI files. But we kept getting rejected.

CHAPTER FIFTEEN

ENTER CLIVE AND BEN

I don't know whether Judge Waldron was feeling bad about executing an innocent man or just trying to clear his own conscience, but he had asked a public defender named Lane Trippe to take my case. She was a very organized, dark-haired woman in a business suit and glasses. We talked for a while. She couldn't take my case because her caseload was already too heavy. "But," she told me, "I know this lawyer named Clive Stafford Smith, and I will ask him." I heard that Waldron had wanted to know if this Smith guy was good enough to handle a capital offense case. If only this judge knew who Clive Stafford Smith really was.

About two months after meeting with Lane, I was lying in bed reading a book when the guard told me to get dressed. I had an attorney visit.

"You got a good lawyer!" someone on the tier yelled down to me. "One of the best in the country."

Death row inmates know their lawyers, and you had all different kinds visiting. One might be from Baton Rouge, another from Philadelphia or New York. A lot of lawyers from up North wanted cases down South because they knew how dirty and corrupt it was down South. If they could prove a man on death row in the South was actually innocent, then that was a feather in their cap. But Clive wasn't from down South, and he wasn't from up North, either. He was from England, which was even better. Folks in Europe were better able to see the broken state of our legal system, and they were shocked by the corruption, often more shocked than people in our own country.

When I got to the attorney meeting room, I saw a very tall man sitting down. It was immediately apparent this guy was something different.

"Are you Dan Bright?" he asked me.

"Yes," I replied. "And you are?"

"Clive Stafford Smith, I'm with the Louisiana Capital Assistance Center, and I'll be your lawyer. We heard about your case and decided to help."

He explained that the Capital Assistance Center was part of a powerful nationwide legal network and had offices right in New Orleans. Clive's wife, Emily Bolton, was also an attorney, and although Clive was British and had a thick British accent, he was licensed to practice law in Louisiana. Still this wasn't adding up to me.

Clive sensed I wasn't feeling comfortable and started talking about some game called cricket, telling me all the rules. I just looked at him, and I thought to myself, man, I don't wanna hear about no damn cricket, I'm on death row. But that was Clive's way of getting comfortable with me, and it worked.

The minute you started talking with Clive, you could tell this guy really hated the system, and he understood what it was doing to us. He knew how dirty and corrupt Orleans Parish was, and not just Orleans Parish, Louisiana period. The South period. Clive didn't like police, judges, and DAs who mistreated poor people. Clive didn't like people who abused their power. He was white, but when he looked at you, he didn't see black or white, he only saw a man.

Before he came to see me, he had already done some investigating. Clive had called my former lawyer, Bailey, and learned about my case. I could tell by the way he looked at me that he believed I was innocent. I told him a little about my past and the drugs.

"I am not here to judge you," said Clive. "I am here to prove your innocence, that's all that matters."

The problem with the legal system in Orleans Parish is most of the players went to college together, they went to law school together, they were members of the same secret societies, they belonged to the same clubs, they ate at the same restaurants, their kids were friends and went to the same birthday parties. And these guys were not going to hurt each other for me. They were not going to take food out of each other's mouth for me. But Clive would. He wasn't part of the good old boy system. In fact he wanted to bring it down. You could see the fight in him. Clive loved a good legal battle. He took high profile cases. He wanted to expose.

"I'm going to put a few more lawyers on your case," Clive told me before going. "You will also have paralegals and investigators." He said that he would be traveling a lot, but a colleague of his named Ben was going to come visit me, and Ben was going to be second-in-command. I felt real good. I finally had a legal team willing to go the distance with me, willing to fight, and I had real lawyers, not shabby, get-your-law-degree-at-Walmart type lawyers.

"Don't look for nothing to happen overnight," someone said when I got back on the tier. "It don't matter how good your lawyer is." But I wasn't trying to hear that shit.

Clive's colleague arrived a few weeks later, and he looked like a 16 year old kid. I went into the attorney visiting room and found this nerdy little guy, maybe 150 pounds, with his grandfather's suit on and shabby shoes, dragging around this big old backpack.

"Hi, I'm Ben Cohen," he said. Ben had grown up in Baltimore, and the Louisiana Capital Assistance Center was his first job as a lawyer. In fact Ben had only argued in court once or twice before.

I looked at him and thought, I'm fucking dead. But when the smoke cleared, Ben was the one throwing all the punches. He was a legal genius, an architect. He anticipated their moves before they made them. We talked for about two hours that day.

The first move for Ben was to get back in the neighborhood. I called home one day and learned he had gone by my mother's house. Then I called a friend who said a lawyer came around asking about me.

"What did he look like?"

"A little kid."

Ben was going around the neighborhood knocking on doors asking questions. This was good news, but Ben was a small little white guy.

"Ben," I told him, "you can't go around this neighborhood like that, this ain't St. Charles Street. Why don't you take someone with you?"

So he started taking a private investigator along. When Ben visited me the following week, he still looked like a kid, but he had a fine gleam in his eye.

"What's up?" I asked.

"You really are innocent," he said, smiling. "I went into your neighborhood," he said. "I talked to a lot of people, and they all said the same thing, that you did not kill Murray Barnes. A few of them told me who the real killer was, but most people didn't want to get involved."

Ben found two new witnesses. They hadn't stepped forward before because the real killers were still at large. But unless these people had a videotape of the actual murder being committed, no one was going to believe two new witnesses from the street five years later. I was happy someone with influence finally believed me and saw things the way they really were.

I also knew that unless we got other evidence, I was still going to be left rotting on death row for a crime I didn't commit.

"So," I asked, "now what?"

"You have some very good issues in your case," Ben said. "But it's not going to happen overnight." And it didn't. It took years. And during that time, I was stuck on death row. As much as I wanted to avoid it, I became part of the life there.

In November of 1999, about three years after I entered death row, Ben filed a brief appealing to the State Supreme Court on relief for my conviction.

"The state stands poised to execute a man on the thin reed of one man's testimony," Ben's brief read, "an uncorroborated identification by a witness so drunk he would not drive. In the entirety of the state's brief, there is not a word of Mr. Thompson's mid-trial acknowledgement that he had started drinking at noon, and continued to drink alcohol over the succeeding twelve hours prior to the time when the shooting took place. Nor is there a single word of the trial judge's historical acknowledgement that he had concerns that Mr. Bright may be innocent."

Ben cited everything these corrupt prosecutors did wrong, 72 instances of error, listed one by one: The jury was given improper conviction instructions; Detective Kaufman's anonymous phone call was hearsay; the state excluded testimony from witnesses that would have shown my innocence; events were manipulated so Christina Davis wouldn't be free to testify in the case; Freddie Thomspon had been drinking for 12 hours straight the night of the shooting, and his testimony was so unreliable it should have been excluded from the trial; there was insufficient evidence to prove the key element of armed robbery; the state examined both Yam and Shelita in a manner that was unfair and impermissible. The point was for Ben to bring to light all the errors the state had made and get information on the record. It was an amazing brief.

Eventually there was a hearing, and after attending Ben and Clive visited me. They were very optimistic. Everyone in their whole office was optimistic. They thought we'd get a new trial for sure. It was April 2000 when we finally got the news from the Louisiana Supreme Court. Ben came to see me. There is good news and bad news, he said.

"What's the bad news?" I asked.

"They gave you a life sentence," he said.

"What's the good news?"

"You're no longer on death row."

"That's good to know, Ben," I said, "but how could they give me a life sentence without giving me a new trial?"

"Because Louisiana Supreme Court found that the state did not prove the aggravated circumstances to convict you for first-degree murder."

"So let me get this right, they downgraded my charge to second-degree murder and gave me a life sentence?"

"Yes," Ben said.

"Don't you know a life sentence is still a death sentence? You still suffer. You watch your family from afar. That's dying right there, it just takes longer."

"I know," Ben said, "but we are going to keep fighting until you are free."

The court's ruling didn't make any sense. I figured they were trying to save themselves. As long as I remained on death row, I'd be getting publicity, so the state snatched me off death row and put me in general

population. They didn't do that out of any legal obligation, they weren't trying to give me justice, they were
just trying to sweep me under the rug. They probably
figured once they got me off death row I wouldn't have
these powerful attorneys any longer. And to be honest,
my lawyers could have left. They had succeeded in getting me off death row, which was what they were being
paid by the state to do as public defenders. They could
have walked away. But they didn't. Ben refused to let
the case go, and he refused to give up on me.

I knew I'd be moved from death row. I just didn't
know when. Everyone knew I was leaving because
everyone kept track of the lawyers. A lot of guys looked
at my case as a victory and motivation for themselves,
that it was possible to get off death row and save your
life. But Phil and Magic knew how I felt, and that I
was still pissed off. We said our goodbyes and swapped
addresses. One morning the guards came. "Pack up
your stuff!"

I went from being in a cell by myself to a dormitory
with more than sixty men, including rapists, robbers,
and all sorts of sick people. General population wasn't
like OPP, where bunks were stacked on top of one
another. You can't do that at Angola because there
would be a lot of killing. Some guys have three and
four life sentences, and they aren't going to tolerate
any disrespect.

I asked around about Goldy and found out he was
in lockdown, or solitary confinement. That's typical of
Goldy. He was going to hang low, he wasn't going to
interact with anyone in this place. And he definitely

wasn't going to submit to Burl Cain's modern day slavery shit and let some backwoods squirrel-hunting redneck tell him what to do.

I was assigned to work in the fields. You are out at 7 in the morning, in at 12 for lunch, back out at 1, back in at 4. If you get thirsty, there was water in a bucket. They had you gardening out there, picking okra, peas, cabbage. But mostly it was chopping grass and digging ditches. If they didn't have something for you to do, they found something, just to keep you occupied. I saw guys with one arm working at Angola and old men. They might be cleaning windows in the dorm, or wiping down the TV or guard desk. Or they might be in the yard goose picking, which means tidying up pieces of grass that are out place and picking weeds and little bits of paper and string by hand.

Angola was hotter than the city. If it was 97 degrees in New Orleans, it was 107 at Angola. And in winter it was cooler. If it was 60 in New Orleans, it might be 40 out at Angola. I could deal with the cold, I could prepare for it, but I couldn't take the heat, and I couldn't take the fields. It was strenuous, backbreaking work. In the summer, it was so muggy you were suffocating. There was a prison law that said unless one of the horses the guards were riding around on fell down from the heat, you had to work. Forget that shit. I took the dungeon, which was like short-term solitary confinement, and where inmates who refused to work were sent. I didn't mind being alone. In fact I preferred it. It was just like death row again, time to myself, time to think and read. I would be in the dungeon for a week or ten days, they'd bring me up, I'd refuse to work again, they'd send me back down.

Eventually Calvin helped get me a job in the kitchen serving food on the line. I stood behind a steam table with all varieties of food and about ten other workers. Guys walked through and told us what they wanted. Sounds easy, but every day was a struggle. There were fights and jealousies but crazy shit, too. One guy with HIV kept trying to squirt his blood all over the beans. Another guy I worked with had a thing for toes. He had gotten arrested in the French Quarter. He wasn't raping people. He would just jump out of trees and suck on their toes. How are you supposed to come out of prison a renewed citizen with psychopaths like that hanging around? Rehabilitation is bullshit. Prison turns you into an animal.

A lot of guys in prison decide to turn themselves out, which means they start wearing lady's drawers and little G-strings and acting like women. We called these people punks, and because they were now ladies, they got gifts like sneakers and better food from some of the guys. Or they might get taken in by a stud, which was an inmate with a lot of punks. But guys could also get turned out by other people. This meant it was not your own decision. You were forced to become a punk. One day there was a gang fight between Baton Rouge and Shreveport out in the yard, a big space with fields for sports, jogging, exercising, and hanging out. A guy from Shreveport had gotten turned out to a guy from Baton Rouge, and the other guys from Baton Rouge didn't like that. Their attitude was, 'If you are going to get turned out, it should be for us, for one of the homeboys.'

The fight happened on a Saturday. Both cities were coming off the field after playing baseball. Some guys from Baton Rouge approached the guys from Shreveport who had turned the punk out, and next thing I knew, it was a huge fight, city against city. Guys were jabbing each other, jugging each other, hitting each other with bats. They were really beating each other, some real gang shit. Baton Rouge was more like New Orleans, city guys. And Shreveport was some big old country boys. I saw one guy from Shreveport jugging a guy from Baton Rouge, and another guy from Baton Rouge came over and hit him in the head with a bat. You could hear the klunk, and there was blood everywhere.

I had come to the point where my emotions were dead. Nothing excited me. I had lost my women, my brother, my friends, my grandmother, all my money, and my life was wasting away inside this slave farm they called a prison. Meanwhile my case was cycling through the courts. But all of them were in bed with the other, from the State Supreme Court, to the Fourth Circuit Court of Appeals and back to the District Court. It was the good old boy system. Didn't matter, state or federal, these courts were all in Louisiana, these guys all knew each other, and all they knew was corruption. None of these courts was willing to address my actual innocence. They were not willing to admit the prosecution did anything wrong in my case.

Every time there was a hearing I was brought down to New Orleans for trial. Usually two correction officers bring a prisoner back and forth to court. I had maybe five or six guys. Two or three sat with me in one vehicle, and the others followed me in a van. I almost always had to spend the night, which meant I stayed at OPP. Back and forth, back and forth. I could be down there for one, two, three months at a time. At least nine times this happened.

If the judge made a ruling right away, then Angola police brought me back right away, but say the judge set the hearing back a month, I had to stay at OPP the whole time. Judge Waldron thought he was going to wear us out. But being at OPP was a break. I didn't have to worry about field work and could lie in bed all day and read.

One problem at OPP was I had to deal with these youngsters. All these guys wanted to do was watch rap videos and the sex channel. You couldn't see anything because the picture was all screwed up, but you could hear the noise. These guys put the sex channel on and masturbated in the day room. In Angola you'd be killed for that. But the inmates at OPP were getting younger, and all these new kids thought about was masturbating. We had a mail lady, and a bunch of them waited for her to come on the tier, and when she came, they started masturbating under a blanket. That shit was disrespectful to every real man in here. You gonna masturbate, go in the shower. Every time I came back to OPP, I tried to put some order on the tier. I'd just look at these young guys and say, "You have no idea what's waiting for you when you get to death row."

In OPP I realized that I had started to know less and less people. The city was changing, and the drug game was changing. These new kids didn't even know my name and that spooked me out. I was no longer relevant. These new guys were less concerned with running a successful operation and cared more about what neighborhood or ward they were from. They were constantly starting shit with people from different wards, creating turf rivalries, fighting with the 17th Ward, fighting with the 7th Ward, the 9th Ward. We had moved beyond that local shit. I was used to dealing with men from all over the city and all over the planet.

"You are fighting the system now," I tried to tell these young guys, "not each other."

They acted all tough, but when they got found guilty, they came to me with questions. The more I learned about their cases, the more I realized they had absolutely no chance, and they had no idea what they were up against. Sometimes there were four guys on a charge, and each one ratted on the other. We never ratted in my day, it just wasn't done, but these guys ratted on one another the first time they got the chance. Then they all got consecutive life sentences, 100-year sentences, 300-year sentences. One guy they called Lucky got 307 years. He asked me, "What should I do?" I told him, "Change your name."

By this point, Ben and I had become real close. It wasn't just an attorney-client relationship, we were friends, and we discussed my case like partners. When Ben visited, I gave him other cases to read, and we debated strategy. Ben brought his findings back to Clive and Emily. Clive was the technician, and he'd decide what we were going to use. And Ben might say, "No, we are going to use all of it." They argued their points and came to a decision. This was the benefit of having a strong team that worked together. Each individual brought something to the table. The New Orleans prosecutors didn't know how to handle this. The DA would be preparing for Ben, since he had written the brief, and the day of the trial, Clive would pop up and discombobulate them. These guys wouldn't know what hit them.

When Ben and Clive came in the courtroom, DAs and judges shook. They knew that unlike the rest of the lawyers in Orleans Parish, these guys couldn't be bribed. They couldn't be intimidated. They couldn't be shut up. Clive was smarter than them, and he knew the law better than them. When Clive came into a courtroom, he had everything, paralegals, assistants, private investigators. He even had his own stenographers, to make sure an accurate transcript was typed up. Law students sat in just to see how Clive operated inside a courtroom. Clive was a tall, commanding figure. Meanwhile prosecutors took one look at Ben and thought he was a paralegal or a student. But Ben ran legal circles around these Orleans Parish DAs. In court I was at home. I felt powerful and important. Now I was ready, let's go to war. I had a real legal team, and I was going to expose their asses.

The DA had to turn their files over to the defense, and Ben searched through everything with a fine comb. He just kept digging, and he kept finding things. Like Freddie Thompson's record. The state's star witness had been convicted of a burglary and was still on probation for that crime at the time of the murder, and the prosecutors had known this all along. Ben was also the one who discovered that one of the jurors was a former Jefferson Parish undercover police officer and current employee of the Orleans Parish Police Department. Then Ben took it one step further. He started going around to the jurors from my case, showing them evidence they never saw in the trial.

Most of the jurors didn't want to hear they had sent an innocent man to death row. But when Ben spoke to Ms. Kathleen Hawk Norman, the jury foreperson, and told her about Freddie Thompson's criminal past, and how he had been on probation at the time of the crime and the DA hid this from the jury, and that new witnesses had come forward to say I had nothing to do with the crime, she started crying. Miss Norman felt terrible. She had sentenced an innocent man to die. When Miss Norman realized what she had been a part of, she became mad, really mad. Miss Norman thought she was living in a perfect world, and this was her rude awakening, that her city was riddled with injustice. She felt that her government had let her down. The word she used was *duped*. Now she wanted to get back at the government. Her mission in life became to see me exonerated. She came to every one of my hearings in New Orleans, and she brought friends. Waldron didn't want to rule with her present so he kept pushing the hearing dates back. But each time he delayed, Miss Norman just came back the next time with more people.

She told Ben about all the unjust things that had happened in the jury room, how the undercover cop tried to push his point of view on the rest of the jury. She also said someone she thought was associated with the prosecution approached her during the trial and warned her that there were bad things about Dan Bright that she wasn't allowed to know, but that after the trial, she should call Harry Connick's office to find out. She talked about the bomb threat, too.

The judge struck the bomb threat from the record, but after Miss Norman brought it into the open, we had a hearing about it, and another juror testified. The state tried to make it seem like they were confused. They said there was another bomb threat at the court-house during the same time period these people were on jury duty, and they must have been remembering that one. But these jurors weren't even in the court-house on that date. "I'm sure that it occurred during the trial," Miss Norman testified. "I'm sure that it was Dan Bright's trial in which it occurred, and I'm sure that we were evacuated from the courtroom." Still the judge said he didn't know what she was talking about. Miss Norman was furious.

She wanted to meet, but Ben said that wasn't a good idea. I had him ask her why she found me guilty in the first place. I was curious. "Because Dan was in jail," she said. Like I've been saying, everyone has this blind faith in the police and the courts. People are being deceived, and they don't even know they are being deceived. Until Miss Norman found out how the system worked, she was all for the system. Once she found out what was really happening, she was 100 percent against the system. I give Miss Norman a lot of credit for that.

Whenever you leave OPP, you don't go straight back to Angola, you go through Elayn Hunt Correctional Center, which is located in St. Gabriel, Louisiana and about halfway between New Orleans and Angola. They have something called the Hunt Reception and Diagnostic Center, or HRDC, where they take your blood, cut your hair, give you all kinds of physical tests, and evaluate your education. It's like boot camp, and you are there for about two weeks. At Hunt you have to walk a straight line with your hands at your side. No talking, don't walk on the grass, don't spit. No smoking. Angola has some of these rules, too, but it's impossible to enforce them. Try telling a guy with five life sentences he can't smoke. There's going to be a whole bunch of killings, and some rapings, too. At Hunt they get away with this. It's even worse than Angola.

Prisoners are traded around like livestock in Louisiana. Sometimes you don't even get sent to Hunt, you get sent to an itty bitty parish prison. Here there is nothing. These prisons don't even have law libraries. Angola guards are rednecks, but they're usually aware of right and wrong. They know the Constitution, and they follow certain sanitary practices. Food has to be a certain temperature, the kitchen must be kept tidy. These parish prisons aren't even up to code, and many of them get paid by how many prisoners they have. These prisons are a scam, built so the good old boys can rake in more money.

When I left Hunt, it was back to Angola. I went from one hell to another. I was losing my grip, which is when you are most vulnerable in prison. It isn't good to start going down that road of depression. You have to take hold of the situation, or else the situation takes hold of you, and you are liable to lose your mind or get your ass killed. If you go around being sad, everyone will know you're scared. If you are weak, every little fish in the sea will take a bite out of you. You have to defend yourself. Let one thing slip, and people will pounce. I needed to be even more wary because my reputation from the streets followed me to prison, and I had to defend that.

One day I was in the shower, and this damn fool from Shreveport was in there playing with himself. This guy was like 6'6, 275 pounds. This man isn't doing what I think he is doing, I thought to myself. But he was, he was looking right at some guy who had just gotten to prison and masturbating. It wasn't directed at me, but he saw me watching, and by doing that with me in the shower, he was disrespecting me, too.

I left the shower, dried off, and put my clothes on, then sat on my bed and thought about how to hurt this guy without killing him. If I jugged him, I might accidentally hit an artery, and he could bleed out, then I'd really be stuck in Angola for the rest of my life. "Stay cool," Ben and Clive kept telling me, "and don't get into trouble." The last thing I wanted was to ruin my chance for a retrial, but I also wanted to survive in here. All night I thought about this problem. I decided to put some locks in a sock and hit him with that, but the next day I looked out the window and saw a base-ball game going on in the yard. I walked outside and picked up a bat.

"Poonie, where you going with that bat?" someone asked.

"I'll bring it back," I said.

I was so focused that it didn't matter if people saw me. I knew they would put me in isolation, but that didn't matter either. I had been alone in a cell for four and a half years, and I knew this much, it was bet-ter than being locked in a dormitory with a bunch of masturbating psychopaths. I put the bat on the side of my leg and walked into the dorm without the guards seeing me. This big Shreveport guy was standing up talking with his back to me. Where should I hit this fool? Fuck it. I tapped him on the shoulder. He turned around. I lifted the bat and cracked him across the front of his face, breaking his nose and collarbone. His big ass broke off running, he ran straight to the warden's office.

When it was over, he was on his way to the hospital, and I was on my way to isolation. This wasn't just a week or ten day long isolation, like I was used to for not working in the fields. This was Camp J, which was strictly for guys on isolation, and where you could be for months, or even years. But after all the time mov-ing around on these court orders and cramped in with strangers at OPP and in these little bitty parish prisons, I was happy to be alone again in a cell.

CHAPTER SIXTEEN

A BEAUTIFUL DAY

I was getting a lot of legal mail, and the mailman was getting tired of coming all the way to Camp J to deliver it. One day the mailman had this thick manila enve- lope for me, on the outside I saw the words: Federal Bureau of Investigation. I signed for the package. My heart was racing. Inside was going to be the news about my Freedom of Information request. Usually you have to open your mail in front of the mailman and shake it out, to make sure there's no contraband inside, but seeing this package was from the FBI, the mailman didn't make me do that and just walked away. The package was very thick, but I was used to getting rejected by the FBI and figured it was another denial. I opened the envelope.

My whole life was laid out before me. Most pages were blacked out, but because it was my life, I could fill in the blanks. These people knew what time I put

my trash out, what color my dog was. They had pene-
trated our organization with a federal informant, and
that agent had followed me everywhere for about six
months. Miami, New York, Baton Rouge. They thought
they were going to follow me to my connection, but
they never got that far. The agent was a woman. I
never expected that.

I got to the murder of Murray Barnes and my eyes
popped out. The agent had been following me the
night of the Super Bowl, and she had seen everything.
The FBI had known all along that I was innocent of
the crime for which I had been sentenced to death.
About three quarters of the way down the page, I saw
the lines I knew could set me free:

*"The source further advised that DANIEL BRIGHT,
aka "Poonie", is in jail for the murder committed by
[BLACKED OUT]"*

I read that file over and over. Before I knew it, the
sun was slanting in through the little window in the
hallway. I lay down and closed my eyes for a moment,
trying to get some rest. But just then I heard a cell
door open. Another guy in isolation came out for
his shower, and while walking down the hallway, he
leaned into this other man's cell and threw shit all over
him. The shit was on the walls, the floor, the ceiling.
This guy must have been stockpiling shit for days. The
whole tier was stinking, and the man in the cell was
trying to clean it up, but it was too much shit. A guard
came down to see what was happening but immediately smelled the shit and ran off the tier to call for
back up. In five minutes, more than a dozen police

officers were on the tier. I had to get out of this place. Now I finally had the ticket.

Still, it was a month or two before I told Ben about the FBI file. Part of me didn't know whether it was a good idea, because I didn't want him and Clive to see everything I was into. Ben probably figured I was just another black guy selling drugs, no big deal. He didn't know how deep it went, and I didn't want him to see that side of me. I was worried what he'd think. But after a lot of thought, I decided it was the right thing to do. I didn't want to chance sending the file to him in the mail, and I definitely didn't want to tell him over the phone, so I told Ben to come up for a visit. We talked about the case. I told him about what happened with the guy from Shreveport and why I was in isolation. He apologized that things were moving so slow and said to be patient.

For some reason, I was unable to tell him then. It was just too big. But some time later, I think it was back at another hearing in Judge Waldron's courtroom, I tapped Ben on the shoulder.

"Maybe this will help," I said and handed him the FBI file.

Ben looked at me. "Dan, where did you get this?"

I explained.

I had bookmarked the page that revealed I didn't murder Murray Barnes. Ben's eyes opened wide when he read that. "This is your way out, Dan."

Even though we had that file, to make our case foolproof we needed to get the FBI to reveal what was under the blacked out part. That took another year.

Another year in Angola hell. Still I was happy lawyers were paying attention to my case at all.

Clive, being the powerful lawyer he was, reached out to a law firm in San Francisco called Morrison and Foerster. This firm is worldwide, with offices in China, Germany, Singapore, Japan. They specialize in cases involving the cover-up of information. And these guys were able to get the FBI to reveal what it said under the blacked out part: *"The source further advised that DANIEL BRIGHT, aka "Poonie", is in jail for the murder committed by JOSEPH BROWN. The source stated that he/she has heard BROWN bragging about doing the murder and how he is confident BRIGHT will be able to beat the charge because they don't have enough evidence against him."*

Now we could go back to federal court and say, look, the FBI saw who did the murder, and it wasn't Dan Bright. Clive took the document to the U.S. District Court for the Eastern District of Louisiana, a federal courthouse located right in downtown New Orleans. On March 7, 2003, Judge Martin Feldman returned a decision: "Given the patent seriousness of the statement, Bright may have been wrongfully convicted of murder even though his prior criminal history hardly makes him a candidate for citizen of the year. The failure by law enforcement agencies to disclose the statement before his murder trial raises the stakes of the public interest and pays little currency to any claim of private interest. Whether Bright is or is not guilty, the failure of law enforcement to act as it was constitutionally obliged to do cannot be tolerated in a society that makes a fair and impartial trial a cornerstone of our liberty from government misconduct."

The judge also criticized the government for taking so long to fulfill my Freedom of Information requests: "Moreover, the government's actions over the past 42 months, as it has sought to conceal the content of document 212, are disappointing...Such tactics violate the spirit of the FOIA and erode citizen faith in government."

The next day another guy in isolation called down the hall to me, "Poonie, you in the newspaper down there."

The article was in the New Orleans *Times-Picayune*.

"In a sensible world, everybody now says, 'Dan, go home,'" Clive told the reporter. "The problem we face is that, although we have proven that Dan Bright is almost 100 percent certainly innocent, the courts, because of legal technicalities, don't recognize that."

Miss Norman was in there, too. "This is tremendous news," she said. "To have someone finally step up and say something's wrong."

She also said the fact that I was still in prison was sickening. "When Dan Bright becomes exonerated," she said, "therein lies my salvation."

The just path was for the State Supreme Court to overturn my conviction and order a new trial. There was also a new New Orleans Parish District Attorney, Eddie Jordan, the first black man ever to hold the position. Connick had finally retired. The best option would be if we could get Jordan to admit an error had been made by his corrupt-ass predecessor and call for my release. Eddie Jordan came from the federal system and played by the rules. If the state didn't have something on you, he cut you loose. Even if he wasn't going to cut me loose, we were hoping that Jordan would ask for a retrial, then we could go back to court with our growing mountain of evidence against the state. But that didn't happen. And the police drove me up from Angola for another hearing.

On May 21, 2003, Clive and Ben presented the new FBI information to Judge Waldron and an assistant district attorney named Val Salino. Salino was scared to death of Clive. He was out of his league, legally and intellectually, and he knew it. He tried his best to tear down Clive's argument, saying that the FBI informant's information was merely "street gossip" and rumor. I found this funny because their whole case against me was built on gossip and rumor gathered from a phony anonymous call. But it became clear Waldron was on the state's side, and a few weeks later, he issued a ruling in the shadiest way possible.

To avoid the media, and because he was so afraid of Clive and Ben, Waldron moved the court hearing from 10 a.m. to 9 a.m. without telling them or me. Of course, Salino somehow got the memo and was there at 9 a.m.

"It's now 9:07," Waldron said, as recorded on the transcript. "For the State and the Defense, I simply read into the record, in the matter of Dan Bright, 375-994, the Court denies the Motion for a New Trial."

This was outrageous. Even though a federal court had stated it was the right thing to do, the state court denied my motion for a new trial. Man, Clive got pissed. But Clive can play the media like a symphony, and that's exactly where he went.

"You don't do these sorts of things unless you're biased," Clive told the *Times-Picayune*. "Never in my 19 years of practicing have I showed up in court to find out that they held a hearing without me. You don't do that in a misdemeanor case, much less a case where an innocent person is serving a life sentence in prison. I'm incensed."

"Basically," he added, "what our friend Waldron is doing is overruling a federal judge. Last time I read the Constitution, that only works when it's the other way around."

So we went back to the higher courts. But we didn't focus on the fact that this new evidence showed that I was actually innocent. Instead we focused on the Brady issue, and the fact that the state had copies of both the FBI file and Freddie Thompson's arrest record, yet hid these documents from the defense. That means either Karen Herman didn't know about the famous 1963 Supreme Court Brady decision and was unintentionally breaking the law by keeping documents from the defense, or she didn't understand the Brady law and was accidentally breaking it, or she knew the law full well and was intentionally breaking it—you be the judge.

Still the Fourth Circuit Court of Appeals denied us again. Nothing new is learned by these documents, they argued. "For the foregoing reasons," they wrote, "we find the trial court correctly denied relief finding that the defendant is not entitled to a new trial." I couldn't even believe it. These guys were just covering for their friends in the lower courts. Like I've been saying, they were not going to hurt one another for me.

In October 2003, Miss Norman filed an amicus curiae—friends of the court—brief in my defense. She also wrote an op-ed in the *Times-Picayune*. Miss Norman was especially pissed off because in denying me a new trial, the court said that even had the jury known about Freddie Thompson's record, it wouldn't have changed the trial's outcome. Bullshit, said Miss Norman.

"To lead citizens into making a decision based upon unreliable testimony, while withholding critical evidence, is patently unfair to the *jurors* and is a blatant miscarriage of justice," she wrote in the brief. "When the jury is misdirected as to the importance of fundamental issues, patently lied to, and given irrelevant and inflammatory information, a fair and impartial verdict is a literal impossibility. The collective or separate decisions to keep information from the jury makes a mockery of our system and turns citizens-jurors into unwitting accomplices to illegitimate state-action."

Toward the end, she really hammered the point home: "If the Government wants to retain Mr. Bright in custody, for whatever reason, it should at the very least not do so under our name, with the suggestion that its own misconduct would not have made a difference to us."

On May 25, 2004, we finally got good news. The Supreme Court of Louisiana stated that "there was no physical evidence" in this case. They reversed the conviction, vacated the sentence, and ordered a new trial.

On June 14, 2004, it was back again to Orleans Parish Criminal District Court, Courtroom F, the Honorable Judge Dennis J. Waldron presiding. The very same judge and the very same courtroom where I had been sentenced to death ten years before. I felt like I had gone through some type of time machine. All this shit had gone down in my life, and here I was, in the same courtroom, in front of the same judge, and he still couldn't look me in the eye. He was still focused on watching that clock.

Ben was there with the rest of my legal team. Miss Norman was there, too, and all of her family and friends. My sister was there with her husband, a new guy I hadn't met before. My mother stayed home. She couldn't handle the stress and possible disappointment. I was in an orange prison jumpsuit, and I still had on restraints and handcuffs. Clive had filled the courtroom with reporters. The local media was there, and Clive had even invited reporters and activists from overseas. He wanted to show them the U.S. legal system.

All of this flustered Judge Waldron. He was nervous, and he was mad about all these people being in his courtroom, observing him, taking notes. "Well this is such and such, from England," Clive explained when Waldron asked him who these visitors were. You should have seen Waldron's face. He didn't like it, but he also could't just put them out because that would be another thing they could write about.

Still Waldron had the audacity to ask some of these people their occupation. They were journalists, photographers, death penalty activists, human rights advocates, racial equality advocates. Waldron turned red. "This is not a racial issue," he said.

"Well," said one of these young guys, "maybe not to you." This whole case had backfired politically, and Waldron just wanted to move on.

"Is the state ready?" he asked.

"At this time, your honor, we'd like to ask for a continuance," said the DA.

They were stalling because they knew they didn't have anything. They couldn't use what they had used at the first trial, which meant they had nothing.

"There will be no continuance," Waldron said. I looked at him in shock.

Clive whispered in my ear, "He has a lot of media attention on him and is just trying to get it over with."

"You have until noon to decide whether or not the state is going to retry Mr. Bright, or I'm cutting him loose," Waldron told the DA and left the bench.

Everyone was waiting to see what Eddie Jordan, the head DA, was going to do. Would the prosecutors push for a retrial date or just dismiss the case? That was the big question. We sat in the hallway and waited for noon. I wanted to go back to trial. I wanted to beat them. I wanted to bring all their corruption out into the open for the world to see. Meanwhile defense lawyers were coming by to shake my hand. The DAs walking by looked at me with hate in their eyes. The police looked at me like they wanted to cut my throat. The media was asking me questions. My mind was in a daze. Noon came, and we went back in. I couldn't even hear the words.

"Your honor," said the prosecutor, "at this time, the state retires all charges against Mr. Bright."

"Mr. Bright should be released immediately," said the judge and left the bench.

After four and a half years on death row and five and a half years in general population—nine years eight months in total—I was out.

"You are free," Emily kept saying. "Do you hear me?" She was hugging me. "You are going home!"

But I didn't hear her. I just sat there, lawyers all around, hugging each other, people congratulating me. I was thinking there was something up with it all, that it wasn't really happening, that there was a catch. I was so used to getting denied by this legal system. Ten years was a long time to be in a cage, it was a long time to be surrounded by negativity. I was numb. I didn't know how to smile. I had no emotions. My mindset was still war. I am going to sue the shit out of these people, I was thinking. I didn't know how to stop the machine in my head and enjoy the moment. Prison does that to you. My mind wouldn't allow me to be happy because I was still angry. My whole point of existence had become to destroy the enemy, and the enemy was anything to do with the Orleans Parish criminal justice system.

I remember thanking Miss Norman, then I was ushered into a police van and taken back to Angola. My sister and her husband followed in one car, and Ben and Emily followed in another car. It was a rainy gray day, but at one point, the sun came out. Clive had faxed ahead a request to Angola, asking them to organize my papers for release, so as soon as we arrived I could be processed out. Usually this process takes two or three days, but Waldron didn't want any more dealings with this case, and he wasn't about to stop a quick release. Clive didn't come with us to Angola, though. He had to stay at the courthouse. Another death row case was starting up. For him a new fight was just beginning. And for me, I was finally going home.

CHAPTER SEVENTEEN

COMING DOWN

I didn't stay long in New Orleans. After being exonerated, I moved to San Francisco for a few months. Ben and Clive thought it would be a good idea for me to get out of town. San Francisco is a beautiful city, with virtually no crime. I remember one day people were protesting on the street because there had been two murders. I was so confused, people protesting about a couple murders? That's your average day in New Orleans. I didn't fit in with that city. So I moved back, and now I am living with my parents. But I am not in the Florida Projects anymore. The Projects are being torn down.

My childhood history is gone. The landscape of my youth is gone. It is better now. People are no longer living in these run down apartments. But the problems and struggles of the Projects have now moved out into the neighborhoods. It used to be you knew where the crime happened in this city. Now the crime happens everywhere.

My parents have a nice little place in the Lower 9th. It is a good house, one story, a yard, and a little fence around the yard. My mother helped raise my kids while I was gone. Now I am catching up with my kids. I am catching up with everyone. I see people I knew from childhood around the neighborhood. I see women who used to be beautiful and now have a bunch of kids and are on food stamps. I see guys who used to play football or basketball at John Mac, now they are on drugs, teeth out of their mouths. Or they have some menial 9 to 5 job, working at Sewerage and Water Board, or working in a convenient store, or in a restaurant washing dishes. There are so many stories like that. People you thought would be successful, who would do something intellectual with their life, who would do something great.

I hold the city responsible because if you are poor coming up in this city, you are expected not to dream. Success for you isn't college or law school, success is a job at Popeye's or McDonald's. Most people settle for what society gives them. They don't think they're supposed to have something good, and so they don't fight for it.

I have had offers to get back into the drug game, but it's not worth it. It's not my world anymore, it's somebody else's, and they can have it. People from my era are either dead, or in prison, or retired. My era is over. My problem now is the younger generation. A lot of these guys I see out on the street have talent but don't know what to do with it, so they become drug dealers. These kids don't respect anything because society hasn't shown them respect. If you accidentally bump into them, or stare at them the wrong way, they will kill you. Young guys don't even look forward to turning 30. They don't think they are going live that long. When I see three black kids in my neighborhood walking home from school, I think to myself, which one is going to succeed, which one is going to be dead, and which one is going to end up in jail? Or are they all going to be dead?

My battle with the state is not over. The Brady issue got me off, the fact that prosecutors failed to turn evidence over to the defense. But we had FBI files declaring my innocence, we had eyewitnesses, we had jury tampering, we even had members of the damn jury going against the state. Still the actual innocence issue was never touched. In the end, all the state admitted is that I hadn't gotten a fair trial. Back in New Orleans, police officers and potential employers will figure I got off on a technicality. People will assume that I am guilty, that I still belong on death row. No one wants to admit that the system is corrupt or broken. I still haven't received a public apology, or even a written apology, a notice in the mail saying they messed up. Not Shareef or JT or any one of the people wrongfully convicted of murder in New Orleans and sent to death row to be executed has ever been issued an apology.

Most wrongful convictions in Orleans Parish are black men, but I don't play the race card. Race is just an easy way to divide people. Racism exists, but we are taught it. When you are born, you have no ideas about race. Take a white baby, a Mexican baby and a black baby, and put them in a playpen together. What are they going to do? They are going to play. They won't act racist. They have to be taught that. Go to St. Bernard Parish, just east of New Orleans, and you'll see the jail is filled with white guys. Even if New Orleans were all white, you'd still need a conviction rate. So black conviction would become white conviction. Of course it wouldn't be all whites, it would be the whites at the bottom, the lower classes. There's always going to be people at the bottom, and there's always going to be people on top trying to squash them down to keep their power.

Power is more addictive than any drug, and the more you get your hands on the more you want. As long as you have greedy men craving power, there will be crime, and there will never be peace on this earth. There are many types of power, entertainment power, street power—what I had—and political power. This is the highest form of power, yet most politicians have no idea what the inner city looks and feels like, which means as far as politics go, we are powerless.

This is what I know: the truth is always going to be the truth, no matter if it takes 100 years to come out. When you tell a lie, you have to tell another lie to cover that up, then another lie. And when people tell so many lies, lie after lie, eventually the whole pyramid falls apart. I remember one time in prison sitting around wondering, why did God give us free will? Did He not foresee the evil shit we were going to do with it? Did He not foresee the killing and robbing and raping and drugs and wars and genocide? Could He not have seen any of that coming? And if He could have seen even one small part of all this coming, why didn't He try and stop it?

I don't believe in hell. I believe you pay for what you did wrong, but as far as that burning forever shit, nothing burns forever. There is no eternal fire. The first level of hell starts in your mind. You depressed, you broke, you on drugs, that's hell. Drugs are hell. And I'm guilty of pumping that shit to people. So a part of me is evil. I made a lot of bad decisions. Yeah, I paid the rent of people who were struggling and took old ladies to bingo and gave needy kids bikes. But I think about the women in the Projects who sold their food stamps to get my drugs. I was part of that cycle on a major level. I always tried to justify it by saying that if I didn't sell these people drugs someone else would. I can tell myself that I never sold drugs to pregnant women or kids. But who is to say pregnant women didn't have other people get them the drugs? And selling to adults still affects these kids because it's their cousins, their uncles, their grandparents who are using this shit. I was part of a genocide machine that was destroying my own people. Not just my people, the human race period. I had a lot of white customers, too. I had my hands involved in destroying a lot of families. I was part of a bigger network that was holding people back, destroying them, physically, emotionally, spiritually. I could have done something else, but I chose the streets because I wanted to be a part of that.

People think poverty is all about being poor. No, poverty is a money making machine, and prisons are where the investors cash in on their investment. It's an easy scam because their investment really means no investment. Make sure the housing is shitty, make sure the neighborhoods are messed up, make sure there are no job opportunities, make sure the police are corrupt. Do all that and the prisons will be full, and the wardens and guards and prison service companies and all these redneck towns where the prisons are located are going to be making money. Meanwhile back in the cities, schools don't even have money for books, other schools are closing down, the roads are broken, the medical clinics are broken, and people are starving and going without heat or clothes. Tell me, how does that make sense?

The average policeman in his patrol car has more power than the President of the United States because they have the power to destroy your life. Say a group of black kids are walking through the Projects, coming home from school, or coming home from the gym, and you have a bunch of white cops pull up to them. It's already in their head that these kids are doing something wrong. The police aren't from this neighborhood, and they don't know how this neighborhood works. The cops have already negatively stereotyped these kids. They might just be coming home from basketball practice, but the police aren't thinking about that, or believing that when the kids tell him. So they throw the kids up on the car, pat them down, check their records. Now you have just made four more black kids who don't like you. Those same four kids you just threw up on the car could have helped you solve a crime, but now they're not going to help you. They are going to be against you. Can you imagine if the cops pulled into a rich neighborhood every day and shook people down? You don't think people in rich neighborhoods are constantly up to something? Smoking a little weed, doing some coke, cheating on their taxes, doing some illegal stock trading. I'll tell you this, you'd see a whole different set of faces in the parish prison.

Being tough on crime will always win you an election in New Orleans, even if it means some of the people you lock up are innocent. Orleans Parish Prison is filled with innocent people. That doesn't matter to the public. As long as a prosecutor is tough on crime in this city, they will get elected. How many of the guys in OPP are innocent of the crimes that they have been convicted? How many guys got put in prison because some prosecutor connived a deal from another guy already in prison? Or a guy who just got out made up some lies so they could reduce their own probation? Deals like that happen all the time, and guys take these deals because it's the only deal this city has ever offered them.

My people are not even using most of these drugs. The drugs are not for poor people. Where do most of the drugs go? The suburbs. Hollywood. The sports world, the entertainment world. That's where the real money is. The average guy in the Projects will spend a few hundred dollars a day on drugs, but people in

Hollywood, or rich kids with their own bank accounts, will spend thousands of dollars on drugs. Famous Saints players bought our coke, and these guys wouldn't just buy a bag of coke, they'd buy a whole kilo of coke. The best athletes, the best musicians, the best entertainers, these people are doing more drugs than anyone. And do you think they will end up in prison, or on death row? Of course not.

In New Orleans, you have politicians and policemen going to prison all the time. That leaves the kids thinking, why can't everything be fair? So what do you think these kids are going to do, especially the kids at the bottom. They look to the top, to these people who are supposed to be role models, and see that they're stealing, and they have college degrees and good jobs. Kids are left to think that this is the only way to succeed, cut corners, make quick money, cheat, lie, deal drugs. If you want to find the root of this problem, look to the top. The people at the bottom are going to do what they have to do to survive. Like I said, New Orleans is like crabs in a bucket.

The other day it was raining, and I was at the little store in my neighborhood. I put my umbrella down as I walked in, and I see this young guy who is always hanging around the place eyeing the umbrella, like he wants to take it. I have seen this youngster before. He hangs out by the store selling drugs. I watched him going to make a move for that umbrella, but then I heard his friend say, "No! You know who that is?" And the friend told him, and the kid backed off. I walked over to him and said,

"Lil' One, where do you think you'll be in five years?"

"Dead."

I said, "Lil' One, why you say that?"

But all he knows is that in his mind he is supposed to die in the streets.

I looked at him real carefully and said, "What you like to do?"

He didn't know. He couldn't come up with one thing.

"There's a problem right there," I told him. "You got to think about what you like to do in this world. I am not telling you don't sell drugs, because I am not going to put money in your pocket, but if you have to do that shit, have a timetable, have a game plan, because gangsters don't have retirement plans. There are no drug dealers running around with white hair for a reason."

A guy in the Projects didn't wake up one morning and say, I'm gonna be a killer, and a paper came for his sister and it said, you're gonna be a prostitute. It's the environment. They have this old saying, show me your friends and I'll show you your future. I say, show me your neighborhood and I'll show you your future. Positive energy rubs off, and negative energy rubs off, too. If you hang around in a negative area, in some form or fashion, it's going to affect you. That's why it's so important to catch these kids while they are young. Give them something to strive for. We need Boys and Girls clubs, community centers, parks, afterschool programs, that's where it starts at. Give the kids something positive to do.

Walk through a school here, what's the first thing you see? Metal detectors. It's like a prison. These boys have to open their pockets, and these girls have to open their purses. Most of these girls have started menstruating, so now they have to let these strangers see their feminine products. All of this shit is negative pressure, just so much negative pressure.

I can identify with what these kids are going through because I am still stereotyped every day. That's why I don't tell people I've been on death row. The radar goes up. People start thinking, why did they put him there? Maybe he is unstable, maybe he is a serial killer, maybe he busted out with some fancy lawyers. And now, why is he back on the street? I try to let people get to know me first, then I tell them I've been on death row.

I used to know a guy with a helicopter, and he would take me up over the city. Sometimes I took Shelita, who loved it, sometimes I took Tyra, who was scared to death. Most of the time I went alone. Once you got up in the air, everything was quiet, you had these headphones on so you couldn't hear a thing. We would fly up over the business district or head uptown. I would see the buildings light up, and the streets light up. The city looked so peaceful from up there. It was beautiful. We crossed the river to Algiers and the Westbank, and you could see ships moving up and down the Mississippi and the cars on the bridge. The objects below looked like they were moving in slow motion. From the top, you couldn't see all the madness of the city, all the murder and violence. It was a totally different atmosphere. Everything was bottled up. The city seemed smaller, insignificant. The ride would last about an hour, and for that one hour, I could forget about the violence. Then I'd come down.

Karen Herman is now a judge in Orleans Criminal District Court, the same courthouse where she prosecuted Dan Bright's wrongful murder conviction.

Judge Dennis Waldron officially retired at the end of 2008 but has continued to fill vacancies at the court when needed. In early 2015, Orleans Criminal District Court Judge Frank Marullo was removed from the bench by the Louisiana Supreme Court after a probe by its investigative arm. The Supreme Court appointed Judge Dennis Waldron to sit ad-hoc, while the court continued its investigation.

Detective Arthur Kaufman was sentenced to six years in prison, in 2012, for his role in fabricating reports to cover up the New Orleans Police Department killing of two unarmed civilians, and the wounding of four others, in a shooting that took place on the Danziger Bridge, six days after Hurricane Katrina. In 2013, a

U.S. District Court judge overruled the sentence, citing prosecutorial misconduct, and in 2015 that ruling was upheld.

Harry Connick retired as New Orleans District Attorney in 2003. "My reputation is based on something other than a case, or two cases or five cases, or one interception or 20 interceptions," he told the Times-Picayune in 2012. "Look at the rest of my record. I have more yards than anybody." As of 2016, at the age of 90, he still occasionally appeared at New Orleans nightclubs to sing, something he was known for.

Len Davis remains in federal prison, though in 2012, during post-conviction trials in which Davis was representing himself, attorneys acting as "standby counsel" filed motions to vacate his convictions and sentence. Their argument was that Davis has a serious mental impairment that renders him incompetent to stand trial.

Ben Cohen presently lives with his family in Cleveland, Ohio, though he still works with the New Orleans-based legal group, The Promise of Justice Initiative, and continues to represent New Orleans death row cases. As of 2016, he was working on, among other issues, the case of Corey Williams, who was sentenced to death at age 16 for a crime he did not commit. In 2015, Cohen received the Sam Dalton Capital Defense Advocacy Award, handed out by the Louisiana Association of Criminal Defense Lawyers.

Clive Stafford Smith now represents detainees being held at Guantanamo Bay and is the director of Reprieve, a legal organization that provides, "free legal and investigative support to…British, European and other nationals facing execution, and those victimised by states' abusive counter-terror policies." In 2005, Smith was awarded the Gandhi International Peace Award. In 2010, he received the International Bar Association's Human Rights Award.

Kathleen Hawk Norman passed away in her sleep on April 15, 2009. She was fifty-four.